the Secret RULES OF FLIRTING

the Secret RULES OF FLIRTING

The Illustrated Guide to Reading Body Language, Getting Noticed, and Attracting the Love You Deserve—Online and In Person

FRAN GREENE, LCSW

FORMER DIRECTOR OF FLIRTING AT MATCH.COM

FAIR WINDS

Brimming with creative inspiration, how-to projects, and useful information to enrich your everyday life, Quarto Knows is a favorite destination for those pursuing their interests and passions. Visit our site and dig deeper with our books into your area of interest: Quarto Creates, Quarto Cooks, Quarto Homes, Quarto Lives, Quarto Drives, Quarto Explores, Quarto Gifts, or Quarto Kids.

First Published in 2018 by Fair Winds Press, an imprint of The Quarto Group, 100 Cummings Center, Suite 265-D, Beverly, MA 01915, USA.
T (978) 282-9590 F (978) 283-2742 QuartoKnows.com

Fair Winds Press titles are also available at discount for retail, wholesale, promotional, and bulk purchase. For details, contact the Special Sales Manager by email at specialsales@quarto.com or by mail at The Quarto Group, Attn: Special Sales Manager, 401 Second Avenue North, Suite 310, Minneapolis, MN 55401, USA.

22 21 20 19 18   1 2 3 4 5

ISBN: 978-1-63159-461-8

Digital edition published in 2018
eISBN: 978-1-63159-462-5

Library of Congress Cataloging-in-Publication Datais available.

Design: Mattie Wells

Illustration: Penelope Dullaghan

Printed in China

To the love of my life, my husband
Dr. James Mullin, for always demonstrating
his love for me and for keeping the flirt alive!

To my mother, Rozzie Greene, a world-class
flirt. I learned from the best. If only you
could be here to read all your tips!
Love you and miss you.

To all my clients and workshop participants.
Thank you for working so hard to be the best
flirts you can be and for allowing me to be
your coach! You have taught me so much,
and for that I am forever grateful.

Contents

Anything's possible if you've got *enough nerve.*

J. K. ROWLING

Be a Natural Flirt in No Time

When you walk into a room full of strangers, how do you feel? Do you think of it as a golden opportunity—a limitless pool of possible connections, like friendships, business contacts, or romantic encounters—or do you find a quiet corner, keep a low profile, and do your best to wait out the storm? If the second option sounds more like you—and even the most outgoing people have moments like these!—I'm delighted you've picked up this book. I want you to feel confident when you meet new people, whether that's walking into a party, attending a conference, or simply meeting someone for the first time—anywhere, any place, anytime!

WHY FLIRT?

Flirting has the power to transform your everyday routines into unique, energizing experiences. Yes, flirting can spark love, but it can also help you create amazing connections in every area of your life. How? First, and most importantly, you have to be open to the idea that every person you meet will add significance to your life, and that every encounter is an exciting adventure. As you become a practiced flirt, you'll learn that some flirtatious interactions can lead to lifelong relationships, while others will be one-time encounters that are priceless experiences in themselves.

Like any valuable skill, flirting takes practice, and, like any sport, it has rules, too. I'm here to clue you in to those rules, and to show you how to use them to your best advantage— no matter who you are. Whether you need a total flirting makeover or a quick refresher course on how flirting can be a game changer, when it comes to bringing more people into your life, this book is for you. Flirting is my hobby—seriously!—and I'm about to show you how you can become an irresistible flirt, too.

In **Chapter 1**, I get you psyched to flirt. You'll find out why flirting never goes out of style and how it can bring joy and fun into your life. In my experience, the number-one barrier to flirting is the fear of rejection. That's totally natural, but I'll show you how to reframe rejection: You might not be able to avoid it completely, but you can put a positive spin on it and turn a potentially negative feeling into a valuable gift. You'll also learn how to boost your self-confidence and raise your self-esteem with unique confidence enhancers that help both men and women.

Chapter 2 is all about body language. I explain why body language speaks volumes about who you are, and you'll learn how to radiate the kind of body language that communicates you are welcoming, sincere, and approachable. After all, when it comes to flirting, it's not about how attractive you are, it's about how approachable you are! You'll become an expert on engaging your flirting interest, and you'll also be able to spot the signs that someone is interested— or not interested—in you.

Online dating sites, apps, and social media websites are the most popular ways to find love these days. So, since you have the technology to meet people online, knowing how to get your flirt on virtually is essential. **Chapter 3** shows you how to do just that. You'll become proficient at flirting via text, online, and on social media; you'll learn when and how to use emojis and gifs, and how to charm your online date into wanting to meet you ASAP.

A large part of your day is spent staring at a screen and typing on a keyboard, so it's easy to forget just how important small talk is. Simply put, it's HUGE! After you read **Chapter 4**, you'll become a whiz at working a room because you'll have your own secret stash of the best "un-pickup" lines and conversation starters. They're fun, easy to use, and will help you establish a warm connection with your flirting interest right away. And, the best part is, you'll look forward to talking to new people, because you'll know how to eliminate that unbearable

flirting-freeze moment—that split second when you clam up as soon as you're about to talk to that hot guy you've been dying to meet. Don't you just hate when that happens?

Have you ever considered flirting at a funeral or while waiting in line at the supermarket, the bank, or the movies? Guess what? You can! You can flirt wherever you happen to be: You just have to recalibrate your mindset and adapt your techniques to the venue. In **Chapter 5**, you'll see I've done the hard work for you: I describe the best spots for flirting, so you have lots of options. One of my goals for you is this: I want you to make a list of all the venues, and then make a plan to try them all. (You'll have a blast—I promise!) If you follow my formula in this chapter for the perfect date, you'll be able to develop your own creative plans for a date to remember. And I've come up with some amazing date ideas that I'm sure you'll love.

MY FLIRTING LOVE STORY

I've already told you that flirting is a way of life for me; it adds laughter to each day, it breaks the ice with new people, and it always makes the person I'm flirting with feel special. (It makes me feel special, too!) And it gives me the green light to express myself in inventive ways. I always have my flirt switch on!

I bet you're wondering if using the secret rules of flirting helped me find love, and I'm thrilled to tell you it absolutely did. Here's the short version of the story. Jim and I worked for the same company, but in different locations (Jim's office was 200 miles [322 km] away from mine). One day, Jim attended a meeting at my office and our group went out to lunch together. I definitely wanted to sit next to this nice, bright, attractive guy. And the stakes were low for me since we lived in different parts of the state. Since I felt so relaxed about it, it was easy for me to be compli-mentary, funny, listen attentively,

smile, and make warm eye contact with him. In other words, flirting just happened! Jim was so easy to talk to, and we had a great time.

Several months later, Jim came back to our office for another meeting. Afterward, I offered to drive him to the airport. Jim replied, "Only if I can take you to dinner"—and, of course, I said yes. As we left my office to go to dinner, a colleague asked me if he was my husband. Jim quickly replied, "I should be so lucky!" I was so flattered and I could feel myself blushing! I quickly responded, "No, I should be so lucky." Well, we both got lucky, and now we're happily married. (Oh, and by the way, Jim relocated!) The moral of my story is, "Low stakes equals great flirting." Be sure to keep it in mind: If you don't project into the future, you, too, will be a fabulous flirt.

WHAT FLIRTING OFFERS

I've taught "How to Flirt" workshops to thousands of men and women like you. They have used the strategies, rules, and tips in this book to flirt with optimism and confidence, and the results have been life changing. They have made professional contacts, landed new jobs, created new friendships, discovered walking buddies and the perfect medical specialists, been turned on to the best take-out sushi places, gotten dates, and found love. And you're my newest student! As you use my techniques, think of me as your coach, constantly cheering you on. You're about to learn to flirt fearlessly and fabulously, and I want you to remember that I am always with you during your flirting adventures.

Finally, thanks for investing in yourself: Flirting is the ultimate way to meet more people—and have more fun—than you could ever have imagined!

> Do the one thing you think you cannot do.
>
> *Fail at it. Try again.*
> *Do better the second time.*
>
> The only people who never tumble are
> those who never mount the high wire.

OPRAH WINFREY

CHAPTER 1

Flirting Never Goes Out of Style

TRANSFORM MEETING NEW PEOPLE INTO INSTANT CHEMISTRY

Flirting is all about making connections, both online and offline. It enhances your life and helps you meet new people. When it's done right—and I'll show you exactly how!—the act of flirting is fun, sincere, and respectful. It doesn't require any commitment or strings, and it's easy to master, even if you're shy, single, or single again.

FLIRTING IS YOUR PASSPORT TO LOVE AND NEW CONNECTIONS

Think of the relationships in your life as stops on a journey. While you're on that journey, flirting is your passport—an essential tool—to finding the love you desire and deserve. If you're a little nervous, don't worry: Taking risks is a natural part of any challenge, but the rewards of successful flirting are so worth the effort. In fact, the first rule of flirting is that it doesn't have to be perfect—authenticity and playfulness are at its core. A first-class flirt radiates confidence, projects warmth, and makes the flirtee feel like the most important person in the room. And, in the pages that follow, I'll show you how to do exactly that.

But first, what's your attitude when it comes to looking for love? Lots of us approach the search for love in a passive way. We leave it to fate, wishing and hoping that love will come knocking on our doors—not the other way around. And we all know someone who's been lucky enough to find love in this way. You might be thinking, "That's how my friend (or cousin, or colleague) met his spouse. If it happened for him, why not for me?" Sure, you might have the same good luck as your friend (or cousin, or colleague), but deciding to rely on chance in this way is often nothing more than a thinly veiled cop out. And I'm not going to let you off the hook! Here's the way I want you to approach flirting: First, you need to start by believing you can find love. Second, you need to know what you want—whether it's marriage,

Remember that sometimes not getting what you want is a wonderful stroke of luck.

DALAI LAMA

kids, a dating companion, someone to share new adventures with, or a great man or a fabulous woman who helps you get back into dating after the end of a long-term relationship. That's half the battle.

Once you do that, it's time to get your flirt on! Think of flirting as an active way to transform meeting new people into instant adventure, friendship, fun, and, yes, romance—and as a way to turn ordinary, everyday encounters into special, memorable ones. And that doesn't just happen all by itself. Like all the important things in life, it takes time, work, perseverance, and resilience, but that's the fun part! Flirting makes the journey exciting, challenging, and incredibly rewarding.

Secret Rule Revealed: Fun Comes First

Flirting is a great way to make a connection, whether the flirtee is single or not. In fact, when the stakes are low in this way—that is, you're flirting for the pure enjoyment of it—the outcome can be surprisingly serendipitous. Here's what happened to a client of mine.

Susan was attending a charity fund-raiser, and she was seated at a table with people she didn't know. Across the table, a guy was talking about his college days at The Ohio State University. Susan had attended a nearby school and she joined in conversation with Brian. Susan flirted with the objective of simply meeting someone new and having a great conversation. She casually asked Brian if he met his wife at OSU, guessing he might be married. He said yes, and Susan replied, "It must be so nice to have that in common." She didn't let her disappointment stop her from pursuing a contact. It turned out that Brian had a useful contact at a company where Susan had been trying to arrange a meeting. Brian said he would be happy to introduce the two of them. Because Susan didn't give up, she was able to turn a flirtation into a valuable connection—even though it wasn't destined to be a romantic one.

FLIRTING WILL ENERGIZE AND EMPOWER YOU

Have you ever been to a really cool bar that's absolutely packed—but where everyone's eyes are glued to their phones, and nobody is even looking around? Next time that happens to you, you'll be ready to shake things up a little, since you'll be an expert in the timeless skill of real-life flirting!

What *is* flirting, anyway? Flirting combines verbal and nonverbal actions to express our interest in or attraction to another person. Flirting is, at its best, playful, lighthearted, and nonthreatening. It's about projecting positivity and approachability through your body language, and it's about reading the body language of other people. When you're exercising your flirting

skills, you'll find you've become a "people magnet"—because you're being genuinely social, you're putting the people around you at ease, and, most importantly, you're obviously comfortable with being yourself (after all, as Oscar Wilde famously said, everyone else is already taken!)

Now you've set the scene for a flirtatious encounter—but when one happens, where could it take you? It's a bit like a treasure hunt: A flirtatious moment could, for example, lead to a shared interest; a lifelong friendship; a professional connection that lands you your dream job; a whirlwind romance; a fifty-year marriage; or a one-time encounter you'll remember forever. And those are just a few examples. The possibilities are endless!

Once you're a savvy flirt, you can approach people you would ordinarily be too reluctant or intimidated to approach. You get to express yourself in inventive and ingenious ways, and set the stage for romantic interest. This is super exhilarating for you, the flirter—but it's also a real ego boost for the flirtee. (Remember, when you flirt with someone, you're paying a huge compliment!) Plus, when you flirt, you feel energized and confident—which means it's the

perfect way to loosen up a bit when meeting new people. That, in turn, helps you break the ice, get into the flow of conversation, and strike up a brand-new relationship. It's good for everyone!

Flirting is so exciting, but it can also be scary. That's perfectly normal! Let's start by addressing your flirting fears and working past them.

CHECK YOUR FLIRTING FEARS AT THE DOOR

We're all human, and when the stakes are highest we seem to end up doing the exact opposite of what we really want to do. Say you see someone attractive when you're getting your morning cappuccino at the coffee bar around the corner from your office. "He's so cute," or "Wow, she totally looks like my type," you think to yourself. What happens next? Instead of making eye contact, moving closer, smiling, or saying hi, you look the other way, pretend the person is invisible, and completely clam up and shut down. It's like your flirting switch gets

flipped from "on" to "off" in a split second. Isn't that frustrating? But the good news is, you can change that reflex. Let me show you how to check those impulses so you can be on your flirting A-game all the time.

"

Fear is a mindset, and so is the will to succeed.

BETHENNY FRANKEL

🔒 FEAR: I'M SCARED OF REJECTION

In my experience, the biggest obstacle to flirting is the anticipation of rejection, which translates into feeling unwanted, inadequate, and unappealing. When the fear of rejection strikes, you start to question your value, and wonder if anyone will ever want you. I know exactly how this feels: I've been there, and so have *all* the people I've helped over the years. And, sometimes, a flirting-related rejection isn't just about the isolated incident: It can bring up the hurt and pain associated with relationship rejection. When it's magnified in this way, a relatively minor rejection can seem a thousand times worse than it really is, because it's a reminder of the pain you felt as a result of past rejections or breakups.

The truth is, rejection is unavoidable. But what matters is how you experience it, and how you react and respond to it. The moment you get that sinking "rejection feeling" in the pit of your stomach, take a moment to just breathe. Tell yourself that although this situation might remind you of your past, you've only just met the person in front of you. You have no relationship history here. Stay focused in the present. This momentary feeling of rejection will not destroy you—I promise!—and, you'll get past it more quickly than you think. The best way to deal with rejection is to be prepared for it. Here's how to minimize the hurt and embarrassment we all feel when rejected.

🔑 SOLUTION: EMBRACE RISK

You've made your move, but she is glancing at her watch, looking around the room, yawning, answering your questions with monosyllables, and you get the sinking feeling she wants to get out of town as quickly as possible. And then, of course, you feel like your life is over and the only way out is to fake fainting. But what's actually going on here? You're jumping to conclusions. The moment you don't get the response you were hoping for from your flirtee, you decide you've been rejected.

Hang on a minute. There could be a million reasons the conversation isn't flowing, and—especially if you fake that fainting fit!—you'll never know if she is preoccupied, not feeling well, not attracted to your type, unavailable, not interested in your gender, thinks that you are out of her league, or has just been dumped by a significant other.

Again, I know a bruised ego can trigger memories of all your past rejections, especially if you're the sensitive type (like me)! That makes it easy for you to let another person's opinion of you affect your mood and even change the way you interpret your own value. Although feeling rejected by someone you don't know hurts, think of it this way: This person has actually done you a big favor. Instead of throwing yourself a pity party, silently thank the person for letting you know instantly that the two of you are not a match. You only invested twenty minutes of your time; you've been saved from wasting two months, or even two years. Now, you can simply smile and move on. That's a win!

> "
> Following your heart means allowing the possibility of finding true love to be stronger than the fear of rejection.
>
> **SUSANE COLASANTI**

But sometimes a flirting rejection has an unanticipated twist. Listen to what happened to my client, Catherine. She showed up for a book club meeting for the first time, and she mistakenly thought the meeting started at 7:00 p.m.–coincidentally, so did Jeff. Since the book club actually started at 8:00 p.m., Catherine asked Jeff if he wanted to grab some pizza. He said no, so Catherine assumed he had no interest in her. She felt embarrassed for asking and, so, basically ignored him during the book club meeting, avoiding eye contact as much as possible. After the meeting was over, Jeff waited until they had left the room before asking her to go out for a drink. Catherine blurted out, "I thought you had no interest in me." Jeff looked surprised and said, "I just didn't want pizza and I was reluctant to suggest something else. As soon as I said 'no,' I wished I hadn't." After I heard this story, I told Catherine she shouldn't assume the only reason someone would say "no" to an offer is a lack of interest. Instead, if someone turns down your suggestion, why not follow it up with, "Okay. What are you in the mood for?"

Now Catherine finally had proof—thanks to an honest new acquaintance!—that you never know what's on a person's mind when you think you're being "rejected." And it gave her the perspective she desperately needed. She's delighted that this encounter had a happy ending, but if she gets the cold shoulder in the future, she will remember this: Not everyone likes pizza, and not everyone is available or interested in a romantic connection.

🔒 FEAR: I'VE GOT REJECTION FATIGUE

An occasional rejection is one thing, but when you're flexing your flirting muscles on a daily basis, the fact is, you're probably going to encounter rejection more often. And that can be tiring and disheartening. So, how do you keep flirting—and, more importantly, how can you continue enjoying the process?

You don't need to let repeated rejection ruin your passion for flirting. You can learn to manage your nervousness so you'll never have to

🧩 *Secret Rule Revealed: Turn Your Faux Pas into Flirtation*

Did you just do something totally mortifying in public? Don't freak out. Instead, use your poise and self-assurance to turn the situation into something fun and playful. It just might be a way to make a brand-new connection!

Let's say you order a glass of red wine, and, as the bartender hands you the drink, you accidentally knock the glass over and spill wine all over the guy next to you. Instead of panicking, freezing, or making a beeline for the door, try one of these options for gracefully turning a near disaster into an outrageous flirting moment:

1 Say: "I guess I didn't have to go that far to let you know I wanted to meet you! I am so sorry."

2 Joke with him: "How about I buy you a glass of red wine so you can accidentally spill it on me?"

3 Introduce yourself: "I'm [your name]; it's so nice to meet you." Then offer to repay him with a glass of wine—maybe white wine this time!

kick yourself for missing an opportunity: After all, fear is temporary, but regrets last forever. I hate rejection, so, just like you, I needed a way to deal with the disappointment and hurt feelings that reared their ugly heads when I discovered the object of my desire clearly wasn't interested. So did my client, Andrew. I'll let his story speak for itself.

> You must do the thing you think you cannot do.
>
> **ELEANOR ROOSEVELT**

🔑 SOLUTION: HARNESS THE POWER OF PERSISTENCE

At first, Andrew was so terrified of being rejected that he never, ever approached anyone at the singles' events he attended. The same thing happened each time: He'd look forward to the event, arrive a few minutes before it started, and then wait around for someone to approach him. When that didn't happen, he left the event feeling angry with himself and disappointed that he wasted the whole night not talking to anyone. He found out the hard way that just showing up to an event and then hanging back and hoping something will happen doesn't cut it.

So, I gave Andrew a goal for his next event: Continue to approach others until he gets "rejected" at least three times. He said, "No way. I'm not going to subject myself to three strikes in one night." But then he realized that if the woman he approached blew him off, the best tactic would be to talk to someone else. He decided to give it a try.

The first three people Andrew spoke to weren't interested in talking to him. He got his three rejections, and was understandably disappointed. He sent me a text that said, "This is insane, subjecting myself to a triple play of disappointments." I knew how he felt, but I told him, "Rejection is an opportunity for motivation. This could be your lucky moment to approach another woman who catches your eye."

Reluctantly, Andrew decided to talk to Kim—and they had a great conversation, full of laughter and playful teasing. He was ecstatic because getting rejected three times had enabled him to meet someone he was definitely interested in seeing again (and so was she!). We had a good laugh at our next session because he couldn't believe I was *recommending* getting rejected. But what was most important was that—with a little help—his resilient attitude and perseverance kicked in when he experienced disappointment.

Rejection is a priceless gift that can save you a lot of time. But Andrew also learned that multiple rejections could help him recognize a genuine connection when he saw it. When that happens to you, it'll really motivate you to keep flirting. So, think of Andrew when the fear of rejection stops you in your tracks. Not everyone you approach will be into you, and that's okay—you want to find someone who is excited about you!

Put yourself out there, be resilient, and keep trying. Every time you take a chance, you risk rejection. You can't change that, but you *can* change your attitude. View every "rejection" that comes your way as one step closer to finding someone you click with.

🔒 FEAR: I'M TOO STUCK IN MY WAYS TO FLIRT

Even the most committed flirt has moments of self-doubt. Sometimes, putting yourself out there just feels like too much effort. Wouldn't it be easier to hide behind your old habits—avoiding eye contact with the cutie next to you on the train, turning down the invite to that party, compulsively checking your phone when you're at a bar or restaurant alone?

These urges are totally understandable, especially if you're new to flirting.

But you already know what the answer is. Change isn't usually comfortable, so if you want to become a true world-class flirt, you'll need to push through these feelings as you develop new flirting habits. Luckily, there are things you can do to make the process easier!

🔑 SOLUTION: USE FLIRTING MANTRAS TO KEEP YOU FOCUSED

Flirting mantras are a great way to stay focused when you don't feel like being brave—when you find yourself clinging to your besties or feeling completely paralyzed, even though you really want to make that first move. Repeat these mantras to yourself to help you take the risk. Think of it this way: At the end of the day, isn't it better to have an "oops" moment rather than add to that list of could-haves, should-haves, and would-haves? Remember that flirting is a sensational way to connect with someone, and the techniques in this book enable you to come across as lighthearted and warm—no heavy come-on in sight. That doesn't sound so scary, does it?

Still, if you find yourself having to decide whether to take a leap forward or stay stuck in your old ways—trust me, we've all been there!—take a deep breath and repeat one or all of these mantras:

- *Taking action will make me feel triumphant.*

- *If I don't go after what I want, I will miss out on endless possibilities.*

- *The person I approach could be the love of my life.*

- *If he is not interested, I can make an easy and lighthearted get away.*

- *Life is not a dress rehearsal, I will make the most of every day.*

Or, create your own mantras! Remembering encouraging phrases like these will minimize jitters and increase your opportunities for success. Store these phrases in your smartphone; write them down and stick them in your wallet; or send yourself your favorite mantra in a (very confident!) voicemail. Then, when you need a boost, refer to these encouraging words.

TO FLIRT OR NOT TO FLIRT?

If you ask me, there's no reason *not* to flirt. Flirting is like a warm chocolate chip cookie for the soul. It will sweeten your day, warm your heart, fuel your body, and put a smile on your face. It will transform mind-numbingly dull conversations—or even no conversation at all!—into fun, memorable interactions.

If you're a newbie flirt, I bet you can come up with dozens of reasons not to flirt. Check out the table on page 28. The column on the left lists some of the most common reasons *not* to flirt. I've heard my clients say all these things more times than I can count, and I'd wager at least some of them sound familiar to you.

But, these attitudes are a surefire way to stay stuck in a flirting rut, and because they can masquerade as "common sense," they can linger even after you think you've conquered your flirting fears. Worse, they're roadblocks that can stand between you and the journey of a lifetime. The statements in the column on the right, on the other hand, open your heart and mind to adventure, exhilaration, and the joy that is at the very core of flirting.

ROADBLOCK STATEMENT: "SAFE IS BETTER THAN SORRY"

When it comes to walking on wet floors, looking both ways before you cross the street, or having sex, sure, safe is better than sorry. But this isn't true when it comes to breaking out of your inhibition zone.

Starting a conversation at the ice cream counter, asking someone for their phone number, or going to an Excel spreadsheet class or singles' event alone keeps you from looking back at your life and saying, "If only I had done it differently . . ." I know it's not easy, but the more you go down the "scary road," the easier it becomes—and the more you'll enrich your social life!

From the Sidelines to the Flirting Fast Lane

❄️ ICE-COLD PESSIMISM ❄️		🔥 RED-HOT OPTIMISM 🔥
Safe is better than sorry.	➡️	Taking a risk brings me great things.
I should avoid talking to strangers.	➡️	A stranger today may be the love of my life tomorrow.
If I wait long enough, good things will happen.	➡️	Make good things happen.
Women who approach men are needy.	➡️	Women who approach men are confident.
Men who approach women only want one thing.	➡️	Men who approach women *do* want one thing—to make a meaningful connection.
Singles' events are the only places to flirt.	➡️	Fabulous flirts flirt everywhere.
It's a waste of time to attend a party where I know only the host.	➡️	Parties full of people I don't know are filled with so many flirting possibilities.
Dining alone screams "loser."	➡️	Dining alone is a resourceful way to meet someone.
I shouldn't talk to someone I don't know until I am introduced.	➡️	The quicker I introduce myself, the more fun I will have.

ROADBLOCK STATEMENT: "I SHOULD AVOID TALKING TO STRANGERS"

Parents should certainly teach their small children this lesson. But you *should* talk to strangers! It's the best way to practice your flirting skills—you can tweak them for future flirting based on the responses you get. Think about some of your routine activities—food shopping, waiting in lines, sitting on the bus, browsing in a store, walking, traveling, and so on. Couldn't all these situations benefit from a little conversation?

Talking to strangers is crucial to your flirting journey. What is the easiest conversation topic? It's what's going on around you. And the more you practice, the more you're going to love it.

Here's a great example from my own life. As I was walking out of a coffee shop the other day, a guy was walking in wearing a New York team shirt. As soon as I noticed it, I just had to tell him, "Since your team won yesterday, any size coffee is only $1.00 today." He was ecstatic because he didn't know about the deal and quickly ordered it on his app. Next stop for me was the bagel shop. As I was enjoying my pumpkin-cream cheese mini-bagel, guess who walked in? The guy from the coffee place, with his extra-large coffee. "How funny is this," he said. Then he got an egg sandwich and joined me for breakfast. It couldn't have been more fun: I met someone new, had company for breakfast, and enjoyed every moment of it! Next time you're hesitant to talk to a stranger, think of this story as your pep talk.

ROADBLOCK STATEMENT: "IF I WAIT LONG ENOUGH, GOOD THINGS WILL HAPPEN"

Who came up with that line, anyway? And besides, how long is "long enough?" This roadblock is probably the most harmful of all. Believing it will give you false hope and increase your chances of disappointment and sadness. Stop waiting! Make a plan, try something new, and take ownership of your life. It will feel so gratifying.

Say you're a regular runner, and you frequently cross paths with a fellow runner you find intriguing. Instead of passively passing her by each week, make a plan to get her attention. Smile the next time you see her, quickly compliment her on her pace, or ask if she's training for a marathon. After all, in life we often only get a single chance to meet someone who "happens to be running by us"— sometimes literally!

ROADBLOCK STATEMENT: "WOMEN WHO APPROACH MEN ARE NEEDY"

The opposite is true, actually. Women who approach men go after what they want and don't wait for Mr. Right to come to them (which, as we learned in the previous roadblock statement, doesn't even work).

Men love when women approach them. I've heard this from hundreds of men of all ages. Not only is it an ego boost, but it's also incredibly flattering. They only have one complaint: They wish women did it more frequently.

I know what you are thinking—*I want him to come to me. Then I'll know he likes me*—but, ultimately, does it really matter who approached whom first? So, why not give it a try? You'll be so glad you made the first move!

ROADBLOCK STATEMENT: "MEN WHO APPROACH WOMEN ONLY WANT ONE THING"

That is so right! But it's not what you think. Men want the same thing women do—to be liked and to make a meaningful connection.

Like women, men struggle with when and how to approach flirting interests, but they know the credo, "Nothing ventured, nothing gained." Still, it is just as nerve-racking for men to approach women as it is for women to approach men. Frankly, they're scared sh—less! So, ladies, give that brave guy a chance. He earned it.

(Yes, there will be guys who approach women only for sex, but that is not flirting—that's hitting on someone. And ladies, if this happens, simply say, "No thanks" and move away.)

ROADBLOCK STATEMENT: SINGLES' EVENTS ARE THE ONLY PLACES TO FLIRT

Quite the contrary! The more you flirt, the better you become at it, the more comfortable you'll feel, and the more fun you'll have—because your goal is to make the other person feel special and important. And, when the stakes are low (you are flirting for enjoyment, not to get a date or phone number) the results can be terrific. And, the funny thing is, it will actually increase your chances of scoring a date. The best flirting moments happen when you least expect them. So, please, flirt as much as you can—you will be glad you did. You just never know where your flirting will take you!

Flirting Faux Pas: It's All About Me

Jason was meeting his buddy at the neighborhood pub to grab a quick dinner after work. While he was waiting for Keith to arrive, he started talking to Alexis. All Jason did was talk about his great apartment, his well-behaved dog, and how he's on the fast track at his job. Alexis quickly said she had to make a call and then disappeared. Jason had no idea why Alexis left so abruptly. When Keith arrived, he told him what happened. Keith laughed and said, "Okay. What can you tell me about Alexis?" All Jason could say was, "Um, she's nice and a very good listener!"

During our next coaching session, Jason realized he hadn't shown any interest in Alexis and reminded himself that, next time, he'd focus his attention on the woman he is meeting. He felt confident he wouldn't make the same mistake again.

ROADBLOCK STATEMENT: "IT'S A WASTE OF TIME TO ATTEND A PARTY WHERE I KNOW ONLY THE HOST"

Attending a party where you only know one or two individuals is an incredible opportunity to meet and connect with new people. It gives you a chance to spread your wings. Take control of your fun!

You can accomplish this by changing your behavior from that of a guest to that of a host. Acting in a "host-like" manner will make it easier for you to talk to strangers. How do you put this into practice? Ask the following questions: "Hi, I'm [your name]. How do you know the host?" "Have you tried the shrimp appetizer?" or "Would you like my seat so you can eat? I know seats are scarce," or "You look cold. Would you like me to ask the host to turn up the heat?" You'll come across as observant and interested in others' well-being.

Don't turn down invitations to parties where you don't know many guests. Instead, arrive early to be part of the welcoming committee. That way, you'll have more time to get comfortable, feel out the vibe, and get to know people at a relaxed pace.

ROADBLOCK STATEMENT: "DINING ALONE SCREAMS 'LOSER'"

Nope. Dining alone puts you in a prime position to flirt with those around you. Remember, it takes confidence to eat alone. It also opens you to the possibility of welcoming a dining companion. When dining alone, try the following tips:

- Suggest to another single diner that you eat together, particularly if there is a wait for tables. Tell your potential companion it will shorten the wait time.

- Comment to a flirting interest about the dish he is eating. Say, "Wow, that looks really delicious. How is it?"

- Ask a flirting interest—maybe that cute waiter or waitress—to recommend something from the menu.

- Bring a book or magazine in case you feel uncomfortable. Props such as these make it easier for others to approach you. It provides a ready-made conversation topic. ("I can't wait to read that book you have, so tell me, what's the best part about it?" "Have you read the article about . . .? What are your thoughts on it?")

ROADBLOCK STATEMENT: "I SHOULDN'T TALK TO SOMEONE I DON'T KNOW UNTIL I AM INTRODUCED"

What are you waiting for? Are you waiting for someone else to talk to that woman who caught your eye? That guy who's had his eye on you all night—are you going to hang around waiting for him to make the first move? If so, you could wait forever.

Wallflowers wallow, but flirters flourish. So, be your own master of ceremonies and go for it. Put on a smile, stand up straight, extend your hand, and introduce yourself. And get excited: This could be your big flirting break!

Secret Rule Revealed: Break the Rules!

My client Melissa always followed the "rule" of waiting for the guy to approach her first. She wanted to make the first move, but was always too nervous to try. But, one day, shortly after she attended my flirting workshop, she decided to go to an art fair and put what she learned into action.

Melissa approached Guy #1. She thought he might be her type because he was admiring an artist that she, too, liked. As soon as he opened his mouth, however, she knew he was not for her—so she moved on.

Guy #2 was standing next to her as she waited to check out the photography exhibit. He looked pleasant, and his friendly demeanor encouraged Melissa to say hi. The two talked for about five minutes until Melissa had to go.

In our next coaching session, Melissa was elated that she finally took the plunge and made the first move. It didn't matter that phone numbers hadn't been exchanged. Melissa had a great time, and her newfound confidence was the most exciting part of it! She told me, "You never know who you'll connect with—and it felt so empowering! I can't wait to do it again!"

WHEN TO AVOID FLIRTING

Okay, I know I've just told you why anytime is a good time to flirt. And that's true, nine times out of ten. But there are exceptions, and it's just as important to know when *not* to flirt as it is to know when to go for it. You should never flirt when:

- **You feel under the weather.** When you have a splitting headache, a bad cold, or are simply completely exhausted, it will be nearly impossible to be animated and confident—two key elements of successful flirting. When you're unwell, the only person you can focus on is you, because you're feeling cranky and sick. Give flirting—and yourself!—a rest. Resume flirting when you're feeling better and are ready to make a connection.

- **You just had an argument.** Anger and flirting are like oil and water. If you try to flirt right after a fight, you may unwittingly react in a hostile manner because the anger you are feeling can bubble up at a moment's notice—especially if you sense even the slightest twinge of disinterest or rejection. Step back, and try again when your mood changes.

- **You feel desperate.** When you feel pressured to meet someone—for instance, when you need a date for your younger sister's wedding, when you just got dumped by your new love—flirting won't work. Desperation is a turnoff: It'll scare off most flirting opportunities, and you'll just wind up feeling worse. When your only motivation is to get a quick fix or soothe your hurt feelings, it's time to take a flirting break.

FLIRTING 101:
THREE ESSENTIAL RULES FOR SUCCESS

Flirting is all about making another person feel spectacular, and it happens when you demonstrate attention without attaching any expectations to the encounter. And you'll be primed for success if you follow these basic—but highly effective, and often underused—techniques.

1 Shine the spotlight on your flirting interest, not yourself.

When you flirt, you want to make the other person feel special, important, valued, and listened to. Your flirting interest should feel as if he is the most important person on the face of the planet. Now is not the time to showcase yourself by doing all the talking or trying to impress. Instead, focus on your flirting interest. Let her take center stage. (This approach also minimizes disappointment if your flirting interest does not reciprocate—after all, your goal was simply to make someone else feel special.) Once you've adopted this perspective, the rewards of flirting are limitless.

2 Flirt for the positive feelings—not just to get a phone number or a date.

I know this sounds crazy. In fact, when I tell my flirting students what I just told you, their jaws often drop. Some seem like they're ready to head for the door and demand their money back! But if you follow my advice, you will astronomically increase your chances of getting both—later.

Yes, it sounds contradictory, but consider this argument: The best flirting is spontaneous and focuses on the present moment. The minute you focus on the future—phone number, date, so on—you increase your anxiety level, you start to listen less and talk more, and your flirting ability diminishes—thereby *lowering* your chances of actually getting a date.

Trust me on this one. Thousands of my flirting students agree that as much as they want that date, they have to stay in the moment and truly enjoy the process to get the benefit from flirting. And besides, as I said earlier, flirting can lead to a variety of satisfying, fulfilling experiences—it's not just about making a romantic connection.

3 Make flirting effortless.

Flirting is a two-way pursuit. Whether or not you return the flirt, it feels good to know someone finds you appealing. So, let the energy grow as you flirt back and forth. Pay attention to the comfort level and interest of your flirting partner to guide your level of flirtiness. If you get the go-ahead, continue. Focus on how enjoyable even a brief encounter can be. If you try too hard and the flirt is never in your court, so to speak, cut your losses and make a graceful exit.

> Confident posture gets you noticed for all the right reasons.
>
> **CINDY ANN PETERSON**

Practice is important here. Think of flirting as a sport: You wouldn't expect to be a good tennis player, golfer, runner, ice skater, swimmer, or cyclist if you didn't practice! Flirting—like any skill—can be learned, tweaked, perfected, and customized until it feels natural.

SELF-CONFIDENCE: THE NUMBER-ONE INGREDIENT FOR FABULOUS FLIRTING

Confidence is your inner guide, your internal belief system that no matter what you do (say hi to a stranger, ask someone out, send a wink online, or text a flirty message) you will be able to accept whatever happens because you know your intrinsic worth, and the outcome of the encounter will not change the way you view yourself.

Have you ever secretly (or not so secretly) wished you were better looking, had a more impressive job, or a nicer body so you could be a better flirt? Most of us have. However, please put a stop to those thoughts. Quit wishing and hoping because those "assets" are far from being the essential qualities of a proficient flirt!

The truth is, confidence is the number-one ingredient when it comes to being an impressive flirt. Self-assured flirts clearly believe they are worth getting to know. They are fearless about being rejected and truly enjoy the playful banter. Confidence is *oh-so-sexy*, and it's a real head-turner!

Still, we all could use a bit of encouragement and praise now and again. And I bet you're craving that infusion of confidence right now, so flirting will feel like riding a bicycle—you just want to get on and enjoy the ride.

No problem! Here are some of my favorite confidence enhancers. What are yours?

Mirror great flirts. Imitation is the sincerest form of flattery! Take note of what your favorite flirts do and copy it. Pay attention to the people who are never at a loss for words and who are always surrounded by others. Observe their eye contact, smile, and body language. Are they complimentary, inquisitive, and having fun? If so, those are the flirts to emulate.

Pay it forward. It's a mitzvah (a good deed) to give of yourself to someone who needs a kind word, a helping hand, a hug, or a shoulder to cry on. Giving feels good, and it has a way of boosting your self-esteem at times when you question your own value. So, when you find yourself doubting your confidence, watch the impact that giving has on you—and your flirting skills.

Say "no" kindly. There are times when saying no to a date or to a request for your phone number will actually increase your self-confidence because you are doing what's right for you rather than just wanting to please others. It's also the most considerate, honest, and compassionate thing to do. I know it feels awkward in the moment, but you're doing the right thing: Thanks to your candor, you won't lead the other person on. Ultimately, the best way(s) to decline a date is simply to say, "Thanks so much, but I'm not available." or "I'm flattered, but I'm taken," or "Thanks for asking . . . I have a friend who I think you'd really like. Can I pass on your number?"

Seek out your cheerleader. Think of someone (a friend, aunt, neighbor, your college roommate) who has sung your praises. Maybe they complimented your flair for decorating; or said that you're the best cook, so organized, so kind, a great catch, that you have the most beautiful eyes, or that you always know how to get the best bargains. (These are just a few examples!) Touch base with your cheerleader. Admit that you need a confidence boost so you'll feel you're worth it when you flirt! Ask for a two-minute pep talk about everything that's special about *you*. (If you like the concept, but feel ill at ease about doing it, visualize the person telling you what you are good at, and bask in the compliments that way.)

Start a compliment bank. Get yourself a jar or a piggy bank and place it where you'll see it every day. Have thirty-one pieces of notepaper right beside it. Once a day, give yourself a compliment. Write it down and put it in your bank. When you need a confidence boost, open your bank and read your compliments. At the end of each month, read them all. Afterwards, you can discard your compliments or file them away for a tough day. Then, start the process all over so you'll have a fresh batch for next month!

Look your best. The better you look, the more confident you feel! When you feel enticing and desirable, you ARE just that. So, do whatever it takes to turn on your inner flirt: Perfect your posture, dab on a little cologne, get a fresh haircut or shave, try a new hairstyle, buy an outfit you feel great in, wear your warmest smile, ditch your worn-out shoes, put on your favorite jeans, and walk into any room as if you are the guest of honor, the person everyone is waiting for. Trust me: It works.

Fake it til you make it. Similarly, social psychologist Amy Cuddy has done extensive research about power (that is, confidence) and stress. Her research has demonstrated that our bodies actually change our minds. She tested the "Wonder Woman" pose as well as the universal pose of "crossing the finish line." In only two minutes of power posing, she detected a significant increase in testosterone (power hormone) and a decrease in cortisol (stress hormone). Cuddy wants her science to be shared. She advocates that before you go into your next stressful situation (perhaps a night out on the town?), spend two minutes behind closed doors power posing! Sound silly? It's not: It's a potent tool. "It can significantly change the outcomes of your life," she says.

GET YOUR FLIRT ON—WHOEVER YOU ARE!

That means you! Regardless of your age, gender, sexual orientation, or background, flirting works for all of us. Everybody flirts (or should!) because it makes us—and the other person—feel valued and noticed. When it's done right, flirting always makes the other person smile. Here's a great example. While I was dining out recently with two good friends, it was raining really hard. When the waiter came over to give us the check, I asked him (in a playful way, of course!) if the restaurant provided umbrellas for guests. He quickly said, "No, but I'll get an umbrella and walk you out." I said, "Aw, aren't you the nicest!" The waiter smiled from ear to ear, blushed a little, and said, "I am happy to do it!" What a great flirtatious moment that was. Being spontaneous brings the flirt out in others. It's all about staying in the moment and making your flirting interest feel great for flirting back.

Flirting is timeless. We all come to the flirting field with our battle scars—our unique life experiences—but flirting is for millennials, boomers, divorced or single, widows, widowers, outgoing people, shy people—anyone and everyone. Perhaps you have just moved to a new city or transferred to another college, or you're newly single and need to create a (new) social life. These things can be challenges, but at any stage of your life you can turn your lemons into lemonade. You can't change the past, but you can make today a flirting success—and the first of many.

Let's get going! Read on to learn how you can use body language to make an extraordinary first impression.

Flirting Is Not . . .

Throughout this chapter, I've used many words to describe flirting, including *fun*, *playful*, *friendly*, and *nonthreatening*. By now, you know what flirting is. But there are lots of things that flirting isn't, and it's important to review them to avoid uncomfortable circumstances.

FLIRTING IS NOT A HOOKUP OR A SEXUAL COME-ON. Real flirts know the difference between seduction and flirting, and they never confuse flirting with sexual come-ons. Coming on to someone sexually usually involves lewd comments or overt sexual references. With seduction, sex is the goal. If you feel uncomfortable or uneasy, trust your gut reaction—especially if you ask the person to back off and that doesn't happen immediately.

FLIRTING IS NOT MANIPULATIVE OR DECEITFUL. Real flirts are always sincere and honest and are genuinely interested in the people with whom they're flirting. Flirting is not about trying to make yourself feel better or getting something at another person's expense.

FLIRTING IS NOT A DEMONSTRATION OF POWER. Real flirts care about others and equally share the power and energy in an encounter.

You miss 100 percent
of the shots
you never take.

WAYNE GRETZKY

CHAPTER 2

Flirting in Real Life

UNLOCK THE SECRETS TO READING AND USING BODY LANGUAGE EFFECTIVELY

Your body language speaks with a voice all its own. Made up of a special combination of instinct, skill, and your unique personal style, your body language has the power to captivate (or turn off) your flirting interest in a matter of seconds. It's what you *don't* say that'll get you noticed and keep the excitement going! With the right body language, you can transform a conversation about the most mundane topic—like the traffic or the weather—into a fun, even electrifying, interaction.

ONE FLIRT IS WORTH A THOUSAND WORDS

Everything you do—your gestures, posture, facial expressions, eye contact, smile, tone of voice, and touch—affects the flirtatious messages you convey (or don't want to convey). Your nonverbal communication speaks volumes and is even more convincing than the actual words you speak. Dr. Albert Mehrabian, the pioneer of studying nonverbal communication, and Laura Guerrero and Kory Floyd, authors of *Nonverbal Communication in Close Relationships*, all confirm that 65 to 90 percent of your message is communicated by your body language. And that means your body language significantly influences how your flirting interest feels and responds to you.

This chapter shows you the secrets of being a first-rate flirt without saying a word. As your flirting coach, I'll guide you through this nonverbal dance so your body language communicates interest, availability, and reflects your self-confidence. Most importantly, you will feel comfortable in your newfound flirting skin, which will enable you to be a natural flirt and to make the first move in any encounter, and increase your optimism about finding love.

So, for now, don't say a word: Just let your body do the talking!

🔒 CRACK THE MALE CODE: HOW TO READ HIS FLIRTING SIGNALS

Every woman I've ever coached wants to know one thing: How can I tell if he's into me? Here's the answer: When a man is interested, he will exhibit a variety of physical signals, from checking his appearance to standing tall and puffing out his chest. (Coincidentally, in some bird species, the male prances around the female while fluffing up his feathers and displaying elaborate body movements to get noticed. If it walks like a duck . . . !) So, if your guy struts his stuff in front of you, you have hit the jackpot! Go for it–his actions are his subconscious way of telling you he likes you.

To get a better understanding of what men do to attract women, try being an "eyewitness" to men flirting with women (other than yourself). Casually observe couples when you're out and about. Pay attention to what the man does and what the woman's reaction is. Take a mental note of what works, and what seems to be the most fun and engaging.

EIGHT SECRET SIGNS THAT SAY HE'S INTERESTED

His flirting begins before he even utters a single word. And that means spotting his nonverbal signals puts you one step ahead of him! Just think about it: The sooner you notice his signals, the more likely it is he's waiting for you to head in his direction and flirt right back!

1 Preening

Men preen–put the finishing touches on their appearance–instinctively. If you asked your best guy friend whether he preens, he'd probably say, "What the heck is that?" followed by, "No way!"–but check out the following and see for yourself. When a guy preens–which means he's into you!–you might catch him:

- Fixing his hair
- Straightening his tie
- Adjusting his shirt collar

- Plucking imaginary lint from his clothing
- Tucking in or smoothing his shirt or pants

The preening man tells you he wants to look his best so you will pay attention to him. Because men have no clue that they do this–it's a subconscious sign of interest–you may want to take this opportunity to

make the first move. Compliment his cologne, his superb taste in clothing, his cool belt, or his great eyelashes. He will be so happy you noticed him.

2 The Eyebrow Flash

When a man raises his eyebrows, a lightbulb has just gone off in his head that says, "I'm attracted to you. Come on over." He may not even have control over this instinctual male move, and might not even know he's doing it. So, if a man raises an eyebrow in your presence, smile to yourself and say, "Yeah, this guy is definitely checking me out."

3 Hands on Hips

When a man stands with his hands on his hips—the Superman stance—he's showing you his readiness to meet. It works the same way in the animal kingdom: He is making himself look bigger and better so you will notice him because he is posing in a way that asserts his masculinity. His stance is assertive and as soon as you initiate contact he will "return the serve." Basically, he's sending you a message that says, "I'm waiting for you."

When you see this happen, walk over to him, give him a big smile, and say hi. Then watch what he does with his hands; once he feels confident you will stick around, his hands will relax by his side.

THE SECRET RULES OF FLIRTING

4 Cowboy Stance

Here, the guy typically sticks his thumbs in his belt hooks or a few fingers in his pockets. This actually sends you two messages: one, that he notices you, and two, that he wants you to approach. This was a common sign of a cowboy's virility in TV Westerns! Men adopt this "cowboy stance" because it subconsciously makes them feel more manly, and more manly equals more desirable and sexy. This signal often goes unnoticed, so watch for it. Translation: "Look at me, I'm hot, and I want to look better than any guy in the room."

5 Wooing Pose

Have you ever noticed a man who, without warning, pulls in his stomach, puffs out his chest, and stands tall? He is sprucing himself up for you! He's trying to portray himself as strong and desirable. By projecting this positive self-image, he's encouraging you to take notice of his manliness.

6 Such a Gentleman

This male flirting signal tells you he thinks you are worth it. Look for the following signs that chivalry's alive and well. Your man may do one of the following:

- Offer you his seat
- Give you his jacket because you look cold
- Open the door for you
- Let you jump ahead of him in line
- Offer to help you (pump your gas, carry your drink, get the bartender's attention)

If you are the fortunate beneficiary of such chivalry, don't let it go unnoticed: Admire and applaud this gentleman and his efforts!

7 The 18-Inch Marker

When you see a man plant his legs about 18 inches (46 cm) apart, take it as a great sign. He is marking his territory, saying, "Check me out," and "Come on over." This is very similar to the way "flirting" works in the animal kingdom, in which the male's positioning often sends a message to his rivals to take a hike—and simultaneously shows the females he wants to be recognized. If you see a guy displaying this stance, don't be afraid to toss a smile in his direction.

8 Room Scanning

When a man scans a room, he is doing double duty: He's looking for available women, but he's also letting you know he's up for flirting. He's hoping you will "catch his flirt" and look his way, smile, and—even better!—start a conversation. If he perks up when he's around you—holds his head high, and his expression goes from dull to animated—it's a definite indicator that flirting is in your immediate future!

🔒 CRACK THE FEMALE CODE: HOW TO READ HER FLIRTING SIGNALS

The men I coach just want me to make it sweet and simple. My client TJ says it best: "Just tell me what to look for and I will." If, like TJ, you're simultaneously fascinated and confused when it comes to interpreting women's flirting cues, you are in the majority! Ladies, take note: Most often, a single flirtatious signal is not enough to alert a guy to the fact that you're into him. He's asking himself, "Is this really happening?" so you'll need to brighten the lights and turn up the volume.

More than anything else, my male clients want a user's guide when it comes to decoding women's signals so they can be absolutely sure when women are flirting with them. Well, here it is: I'm about to give you a user's guide of your very own!

First of all, women are much subtler than men when it comes to attracting potential partners. Their actions are typically a bit more complicated and, therefore, slightly more difficult to decode. But I'll show you how to read the signs quickly and accurately– and that'll show you how to make the perfect move.

To kick things off, I'd like you to do the same exercise on page 46– observe men and women flirting. Watch them interact; see what the women do to get a positive response from men. Do they laugh at what their guy says? Do they keep tucking their hair behind their ears? Do they fidget with bracelets or necklaces? These may all be signs they're trying to get–and hold–his attention!

🧩 Secret Rule Revealed: Perfect Your People-Watching Skills

I know, I know: You might be thinking, "Watching people? But I don't want them to think I am spying on them!" Not to worry: You're not, and there are plenty of opportunities to subtly observe flirting in action (FIA). All you need to do is keep your eyes open. Some of my favorite examples of FIA include couples dining together, standing at a bar, waiting in line, sitting next to each other at a party, or chatting on the bus or subway. All it takes is a little tuning in of the senses and you'll be amazed by what you notice and, even better, you'll pick up some great tips!

Renee was at a party where she barely knew anyone. She was sitting by herself getting bored with no one to talk to so she put on some lipstick, fixed her hair, and reapplied her perfume. She thought to herself, "I feel better now." Joey walked by and said, "Wow, you smell great." Renee said, "Thanks!" and playfully offered him her wrist so he could get another whiff. They both chuckled and a fun, uplifting conversation followed.

EIGHT SECRET WAYS TO KNOW SHE'S INTERESTED

The best way to determine whether a woman is interested in you is to know which signals women most often display when they want to catch your eye. If you receive one or more of these signs, it's your cue to seize the moment and flirt back.

1 Hair Play

Women love to play with their hair. If you see her run her fingers through her hair, fluff up her hair, or rearrange it so it looks perfect, take notice. If she does this while she thinks you are checking her out, approach her and tell her what great hair she has (or start any sort of conversation). In all likelihood, she'll enjoy that you made a move.

2 The Head Toss

You've definitely seen the head toss—you know, when a woman flings her hair back as she raises her head. It's all about getting you to pay attention to her. A woman's hair is her most valuable accessory. So, when she tosses it, pay attention.

3 Exposed Wrists

A woman's wrists are a sensual body part. That means a woman who gently pushes up her sleeves (if she has any) and plays with her watch or bracelet wants you to know she is open to you.

4 The Shoe Dangle

The flirting woman dangles her high heels off her foot while seated on a bar stool or high chair. This draws attention to her legs in a playful way. Often, she does this in conjunction with crossing her legs—and she may be unaware she's doing either one!

5 Crossing and Uncrossing Her Legs

If she slowly and delicately crosses and uncrosses her legs, this woman is sending a very clear message that she wants you to notice her.

6 Playful Touching

When a woman finds excuses to touch you, it's a clear sign she is flirting with you. Women touch men they are interested in. If she taps your arm, touches your hand, gives you a high five, or lets her foot find yours, she is definitely attracted to you!

7 Chuckling at Your Jokes!

The more a woman laughs at your jokes or giggles when you say something (even if it's not that funny), it's a sure sign she is flirting with you. It says she loves getting to know you and being around you.

8 Gussying Up

A primping woman cares about how she looks—not only for herself, but also to impress you. If she does any of the following while looking at you, or returns from the ladies' room with a fresh coat of lipstick, it's your lucky day—she's doing it solely for you!

- Spritzes perfume
- Shifts her blouse
- Tucks her hair behind her ear
- Plays with her earrings
- Repositions her necklace or a bracelet

These are your cues to approach her and compliment her.

SAY CHEESE: SMILING MAKES YOU MORE ATTRACTIVE AND APPROACHABLE

A smile is to flirting what air is to breathing–without it, flirting is impossible. Your warm and radiant smile sets the stage for a great flirtatious encounter. In a study conducted by Kelton Global on behalf of the American Academy of Cosmetic Dentistry, many Americans reported that, more than anything else, it's a person's smile they remember after first meeting.

Here's why. Smiling is one of the most valuable ingredients in your flirting repertoire. It lights up your face and truly changes your appearance. Your smile will draw people in and make them feel welcome in your presence. A genuine smile says, "I like you, I accept you, and, yes, I want to meet you." A 2014 study published in the *Journal of Cognition and Emotion* found that when asked who they find most attractive, both men and women selected pictures of smiling people. This means it's all about approachability: The more approachable you are, the greater your chances will be of connecting with a romantic partner.

And this doesn't just work for potential love connections: In any social or work situation, you may either want to get noticed, make the first move, or both. Smiling is the perfect way to signal your approachability.

Just in case you need more reasons to smile, here are my favorites!

Smiling releases endorphins. As you move the muscles in your face to smile, your brain releases chemicals called endorphins, which reduce stress and increase feelings of happiness.

Smiling increases your comfort zone. Staying in your comfort zone feels safe, right? Well, a study has shown that smiling will decrease your need for the familiar and will increase your level of comfort when you feel ill at ease.

Smiling boosts your immune system. The more you smile, the more white blood cells your body produces. This is your body's way of fighting infections.

Smiling enhances your trustworthiness. Smiling makes you appear more trustworthy–a valuable asset when it comes to flirting.

THE BEST SMILE IS YOUR REAL SMILE

It's as simple as that. And there's a good reason for it. Your real smile—also known as the Duchenne smile, after the nineteenth-century French neurologist who identified different smile types—involves both your mouth and your eyes, and it's natural, relaxed, and genuine. An authentic smile spans your whole face, starting with the laugh lines around your eyes, moving through your dimples, and spreading across your cheeks and lips. It sends a powerful message: A smile is the universal signal for friendliness.

On the other hand, a quick smile that drops away fast communicates insincerity.

If smiling makes you self-conscious, that's okay. You can overcome this by paying attention to your reaction when a stranger smiles at you. If you are anything like me, I feel terrific when someone smiles at me. So, there's no need to be nervous: When you smile at someone, you improve his or her day!

When Life Throws You a Curveball

Ann Marie, a widow of one year, was ready to meet new people. "I never imagined that I would ever be back out there dating again!" she told me. At first, just the thought of it terrified her. "After my session with Fran, I decided I would practice smiling at strangers. On Day 1, I could barely get my lips to move. I felt so uneasy and uptight. But by Day 4, it already felt doable! It actually made me feel better and more alive."

PRACTICE MAKES (A SMILE) PERFECT

If smiling at people feels unnatural, or if you just want to perfect your smile, practice smiling at people during everyday encounters. For example, smile while walking your dog, waiting for a bus, or standing in line at the supermarket, pharmacy, or coffee shop.

Need a little more guidance? Here's exactly what to do: Look at the person for approximately two to four seconds, smile, look away, and then continue on your way. Remember, there are no strings attached. There's no obligation to start a conversation. Just smile. Practice this technique twice a day for two weeks: The more you do it, the more comfortable you'll feel, and the more automatic it will become.

MAKE EYE CONTACT TO ESTABLISH TRUST AND INTIMACY

Imagine seeing someone who looks interesting to you. Now, what do you do? You could look away for a few seconds—and then, by the time you are ready to do something about it, he's gone. Alternatively, you could wait for him to approach you, which may never happen. Isn't there a better way to show you're intrigued? Yes, there is!

Show that he has captured your attention by making eye contact and looking directly into his eyes. It helps forge a connection and can actually make you come across as more attractive!

EYE CONTACT DISPLAYS SELF-CONFIDENCE

Eye contact is the soul of flirtation: It's a great way to introduce yourself to your interest. (Remember, eye contact should last two to four seconds. Anything longer will cause the other person to feel uncomfortable.) Plus, making eye contact is a sign of self-confidence, which is a real turn-on. There will be times when your self-esteem bottoms out and all you want to do is avoid eye contact. Don't give in! You're worth it, and the more you show this to others, the greater your chances are for success.

EYE CANDY: SECRET TECHNIQUES FOR GIVING THE BEST "FLIRTING EYE"

As with any other skill, to become comfortable making eye contact, you must practice. Whatever you do and wherever you are, make eye contact: in an elevator, a bookstore, a restaurant, a class, on the street, in a church or temple, in a park–everywhere.

Try these techniques next time you want to meet the eyes of a stranger!

◉ Glance, Then Look Away

Glance at your flirting interest for one to two seconds and then look away. Repeat two or three times. Once you've mastered this, glance at your crush for two to three seconds and then look away. Repeat several times. This is a perfect move when you are in a large group, when you're

Secret Rule Revealed: Your Eyes Say It All

Did you know that your eyes flirt without you realizing it? Your pupils dilate when you come in contact with someone you like.

across the room from your flirting interest, or during situations where being quiet is the norm (like a class or theater performance).

👁 Master the Darting Eye Glance

Men are naturals at performing the darting eye glance, and women can be great at it, too. Try it; you'll love it! Here's what men do: They look at a woman, look away, look again, and look away. It all happens quickly; one round of four glances takes no more than five seconds. The man often does this without even thinking when he is attracted to a woman. If you receive the darting eye glance, respond with a smile and a glance, and slowly move closer to him.

👁 Initiate the Look-Down Eye Glance

Women are experts at this technique. They look at a man for one second and then immediately look down. They repeat this several times. Any guy lucky enough to receive the look-down technique can be 99 percent sure this woman wants his attention. If you receive the look down, opportunity is knocking. Respond with an open smile.

👁 Wink to Create a Secret

Want a natural way to create intimacy? Try winking. It takes only a second, it creates a very private and playful way of connecting—and it's sexy, too.

🧩 Secret Rule Revealed: Use the Eye-Contact Trick

If looking at someone directly in the eyes is too nerve-racking for you, focus your eye contact on the person's forehead or chin. This technique gives your flirting partner the impression of eye contact—and you won't feel nearly as nervous.

Winking at someone establishes, in a nonverbal way, a special bond between you. This simple action, once considered in the male domain, has become a gender-neutral signal. A woman who winks at a guy will definitely grab his attention! A wink coupled with a winning smile is a home run.

A perfect wink happens just once. Look at your flirting interest, get his or her attention, and quickly close one eyelid (whichever eye feels most comfortable and natural).

To practice before taking your wink "to the field," try winking at yourself in the mirror or asking a friend to wink at you (and wink back).

DITCH THESE TYPES OF EYE CONTACT: DOOMED FOR DISAPPOINTMENT

✖ **Prolonged eye contact**. Your flirting interest will perceive this as threatening and intrusive, and she probably won't stick around because it feels uncomfortable.

✖ **Passive eye contact**. Here, you barely look at your flirting interest, but focus on everything else instead. Not a good idea! It conveys disinterest or dishonesty on your part, and that is absolutely not what you want.

🧩 Secret Rule Revealed: The Warmth of Your Winking Eye

Sasha was quite reluctant to consider winking, although she loved the idea. But the thought of *her* winking at a guy just seemed too weird. "I could never do that; it seems too pushy," she said. Sasha wanted to overcome her fear, so she decided to wink randomly at the four-year-olds at her friend's daughter's birthday party. Their giggles and acceptance gave her the confidence to try it with men, who were also quite receptive!

✖ No eye contact at all. If you are talking to someone and, literally, make zero eye contact (that is, you look at the floor or ceiling), she will be gone before you finish your first sentence. It's a huge turn-off.

✖ Creepy eye–body contact. After you make eye contact or wink, whatever you do, don't stare or roll your eyes up and down the other person's body. That's plain creepy!

Eye contact should feel friendly and relaxed and should never come across as hostile, intrusive, or disinterested. "Easy on the eyes" is more than a great saying–it's a great tip, too!

YOUR FLIRTATIOUS HANDSHAKE WILL MAKE AN EXTRAORDINARY FIRST IMPRESSION

The flirtatious handshake is the most playful, interesting move you can have in your flirting repertoire! Once you master it, you will always (and forever) make an unforgettable first impression. Let me explain how.

This handshake captivates your flirting interest because the connection comes from your smile, your eyes, and an engaging touch that leaves the recipient speechless–just for a moment–and eager to get to know you.

The Power of the Female Flirtatious Handshake

Nancy went to a 50th birthday party and used the female flirtatious handshake to introduce herself to Jonathan, a guy she just *had* to meet. Jonathan, now her boyfriend, later told Nancy that the thrill, warmth, and element of surprise in her handshake made for an incredible icebreaker.

THE SENSORY FACTOR OF THE FEMALE FLIRTATIOUS HANDSHAKE

Ladies, here are five steps to learning this fun, flirty handshake. Take a deep breath, stand up straight, and let your outrageousness shine! As you approach that charming man, do the following (in the order listed here):

- Smile.

- Look directly into his eyes.

- Move in toward him and extend your right hand to initiate a handshake.

- With your right hand, shake his right hand with a firm grip. Simultaneously, using your left hand, quickly, softly, and gently stroke the back of his hand (the one you're holding).

- Say, "Hi, I'm [your name]. It's so nice to meet you!" (The bigger the smile the better.)

WINNING REASONS TO USE THE FEMALE FLIRTATIOUS HANDSHAKE

Why use this inviting handshake instead of the polite, standard "businessy" one? Because it says the following loud and clear:

- I want to wow you!

- I dare to be unique.

- I want you to know I have noticed you.

As with all your flirty tools, the more you practice this handshake, the more comfortable you'll be with it, and the more confident you'll feel using it. Have fun with it, and remember to keep it lighthearted and playful. Feel free to modify it if it doesn't feel right for you (but not until you have tried it a few times—promise me that!).

THE SENSORY FACTOR OF THE MALE FLIRTATIOUS HANDSHAKE

Guys, here are five easy steps to learn this enticing handshake. Remember, confidence is your ticket to success. As you approach that spectacular woman, do the following (in the order listed here):

• Smile.

• Look directly into her eyes.

• Move in toward her and extend your right hand to initiate a handshake.

• With your right hand, shake her right hand as you normally would. Simultaneously, bring your left hand into the shake and give an extra squeeze to the back of her hand (the one you're holding). Think of your hands as the bread of a sandwich, with her hand as the filling.

• Say Hi, "I'm [your name]. Very glad to meet you."

HOW TO FLIRT WITH THE IDEAL AMOUNT OF PERSONAL SPACE

Have you ever found yourself literally backing up as someone talks to you? You do it instinctively to re-establish comfortable boundaries. "How creepy," you think–and how exasperating that the "close talker" doesn't get the hint. An astute flirt NEVER gets closer than an arm's length from his or her flirting interest.

When you invade someone else's space, that person will do whatever is necessary to maintain comfort and safety. Getting too close, no matter how innocent your behavior, can turn someone off–exactly the opposite effect you're hoping for!

BILLBOARDS THAT SAY YOU'RE TOO CLOSE FOR COMFORT

Be on the lookout for any of the following nonverbal clues that scream you are too close to your flirting interest:

- He leans back.
- She moves her chair away from you.
- He looks over you to avoid eye contact.
- She folds her arms in front of her.

- He leans his chin down and scrunches his shoulders into his neck.

If you notice any of these signals, casually take a step or two backward to reestablish a flirty vibe. Watch how much better your flirting interest reacts. But if, after a few minutes, your crush's reaction doesn't change, take note: It might be time to move on to a new flirting partner.

🔒 UNLOCK THE FLIRTING ZONES: THE KEY TO FINDING THE PERFECT DISTANCE

Great flirts always pay attention to the following flirting zones. Think of flirting zones as the street signs of flirting: They keep you on track, help you win over your flirting interest, and ultimately bring you closer because you respect the other person's space.

Remember, it is much better to be invited to move closer than to get pushed away!

◀···· **18"** ····▶
(46 cm)

THE DO-NOT-FLIRT ZONE

This zone is the space 18 inches (46 cm) out from your body, space normally reserved for whispering, hugging, or getting quite cozy!

As such, moving into the Do-Not-Flirt Zone is an absolute no-no for first-time flirters. If you enter this zone, you will likely get the boot before you can say a word.

THE BEST FLIRTING ZONE

This zone, approximately 18 inches (46 cm) to 4 feet (1.2 m) from your interest, is the ideal flirting distance. You can easily see each other's non-verbal cues, and it allows you to comfortably talk, make eye contact, and get checked out!

When approaching someone, start at 3 to 4 feet (1 to 1.2 m) away. As the flirting progresses, slowly move in closer—but only when it feels right and your flirting interest gives you cues, such as saying, "I'm having trouble hearing you," or motioning for you to get closer!

Secret Rule Revealed: Know Your No-Zone

To figure out your space boundaries, have a friend walk toward you. When you feel uncomfortable say, "Stop." The distance between you and your friend is your comfort zone. Everyone's boundaries differ, so return the favor and have your friend give it a try.

THE FLIRTING-AT-A-DISTANCE ZONE

This is 4 to 10 feet (1.2 to 3 m) away from your flirting interest, and equals flirting across the room or street. Your flirting moves have to be direct to get you noticed in this zone—but it is possible. Make eye contact, send over a drink, wink, smile, and eventually make your way over to the person who sparked your interest.

HOW TO PORTRAY FIRST-CLASS BODY LANGUAGE

The right body language can spark interest, attraction, and acceptance; the wrong body language can trigger discomfort, dislike, or rejection. You probably know people with a knack for making you feel special and comfortable and others who quickly make you feel self-conscious, uneasy, and unworthy. You intuitively react to their body language, which then translates into how you feel about yourself and the other person.

By learning to read and control your body language, you can ensure you give off signals that communicate to others your authenticity, warmth, and spirit. Plus, you'll also know when your interest doesn't reciprocate your feelings—an enormous long-term benefit that will save you time, energy, and heartache. (You just have to trust me on that one, no matter how much you want to disregard the warning signs!)

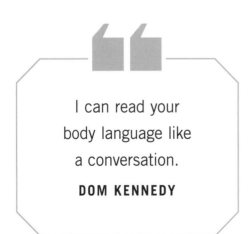

I can read your body language like a conversation.

DOM KENNEDY

BODY LANGUAGE TO AVOID

Before I tell you about the perfect body language formula, let's consider what *not* to do. The Ultimate Body Language Turn-Offs list may look long, but we turn to many of these behaviors out of habit or even without being aware we are doing them. Sometimes, we even do these things *on purpose* to indicate to others we're not interested—so be on the lookout for both! Don't follow these bad habits, and don't waste your time with people who do.

Remember, these turn people off, are unattractive, and stand in your way when it comes to establishing a connection with someone.

The Ultimate Body Language Turn-Offs

- Looking around the room when talking
- Looking at the floor when talking
- Staring when talking
- Checking your cell phone, watch, or fitness tracker
- Speaking in a monotone or so low that your flirting interest can't hear you
- Speaking in a loud, arrogant tone of voice
- Covering your mouth
- Laughing excessively (or at inappropriate times)
- Plastering a smile on your face
- Frowning or grimacing
- Nodding a mile a minute
- Shuffling your feet
- Standing or sitting in a slumped position
- Standing like a statue
- Leaning way back or barely facing your flirting interest
- Getting too close too quickly
- Folding your arms across your chest in a tight, clenched manner
- Shaking your knee or legs
- Picking at your skin
- Pinching or rubbing your nose
- Rubbing your earlobes, arms, or legs
- Sighing, yawning, or rubbing your throat
- Wringing your hands
- Shaking hands with a limp handshake

TURN YOUR WRONGS INTO RIGHTS

Now that you know the turn-offs, what's next? First, take a look at the list on page 69 and check off the behaviors you are guilty of. (Don't beat yourself up: We've all done some of these things!)

For most of the turn-offs, what to do is this: Simply don't do them. For some, do the opposite. For example, instead of slouching, stand up straight. Instead of glancing at your watch, make eye contact with your conversation partner. When you catch yourself mumbling or speaking too low, speak up.

There's no need to be too vigilant, though. An occasional yawn, sigh, or nervous gesture is totally normal. It's when you either express or receive clusters of these turn-offs that they become significant.

YOUR BODY SPEAKS ITS OWN LANGUAGE: IT MAY DIVULGE MORE THAN YOU THINK

Now that we've covered what *doesn't* work, let's figure out how to get you noticed and keep the spark alive with inviting body language. Have you ever tried to hide your excitement or pretend you liked someone when you didn't? (I can't!) Since our nonverbal communication leaks out to expose our true feelings, the more you know how to communicate your interest, the better skilled you will be when it comes to expressing your attraction to someone. Welcoming body language makes others feel comfortable around you and shows others you feel good about yourself. Here's everything you need to do to keep things moving forward.

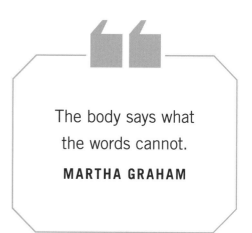

The body says what
the words cannot.

MARTHA GRAHAM

FACE THE PERSON DIRECTLY AND MAKE EYE CONTACT

When engaged in conversation, face the person you are talking to. This sends the message that you are totally absorbed in what she has to say. In situations where it is physically difficult to face each other, such as a crowded event or waiting area, angle your body toward your flirting interest as much as possible, but avoid being overwhelmingly close. Next, focus your eyes—gently. Engaging eye contact works best here. Nothing is more distracting than squinting or straining eyes. It makes you look as if you are trying way too hard, and it's basically just strange!

LEAN IN

Leaning toward your flirting interest says you are into him! When you lean in, you block out the world. You're saying only he matters right now. Try leaning in, talking, and then leaning in a little more.

DISPLAY WELCOMING ARMS

Have your arms in an open position—that is, relaxed at your sides. They don't have to remain completely still, but they should make only smooth, natural moves. Avoid crossing your arms or clutching them tightly against your body. This closed position makes others think you aren't interested in conversation (even if you really are). Arms in an open position tell others you would like them to join you.

I speak two languages, body and English.

MAE WEST

TILT YOUR HEAD

Tilting your head toward your flirting interest says you are interested. It demonstrates curiosity and indicates you really want to hear what the other person has to say. This will be an ego boost for your flirting interest, and, in turn, she will likely let her guard down and feel more relaxed. Like all forms of flirting, body language is all about reducing anxiety, increasing spontaneity, and focusing on the moment.

LISTEN ATTENTIVELY AND EXTEND YOUR UNDIVIDED ATTENTION

Ignore distractions, tune out others, and listen twice as much as you speak. The best way to listen attentively is to nod every few seconds, making comments such as "uh-huh," "mmm," "yes, definitely," "absolutely," and so on—in a natural way, of course.

It may sound obvious, but this guarantees great results. There is no better feeling than knowing that someone truly hears you.

Multitasking has become the norm, but during a first-time meeting, it's imperative that your flirting interest has your undivided attention.

TUNE IN TO THE MOST TRUTHFUL PART OF YOUR BODY

We can hide our emotions in all body parts except our feet and legs. Some experts believe that because our feet are the farthest body part from the brain, they don't think—they just *do*. We point our legs toward our flirting interest. Otherwise, we point our legs away. If you can't decide whether he likes you, look at the direction of his feet—they'll tell you the truth.

USE THE RIGHT TOUCH TO ESTABLISH A CONNECTION

Touching can be your one-way ticket to flirting paradise—or flirting misery. When it comes to this flirting move, remember that less is so much better than more. A gentle, appropriate touch can generate instant rapport and connection. It can soothe and melt away flirting jitters. It is a crystal-clear sign of attraction and interest.

Too much touching, touching too soon, or touching the wrong body parts, however, will instantly turn off your flirting interest. Once that happens, it is virtually impossible to restart the flirting dance, especially if the woman feels threatened. If a man's touch comes off as creepy, the woman will do anything to get away as quickly as possible. Both men and women need to respect their flirting interests' boundaries.

So, pay close attention to the reaction when you casually—accidentally or purposely—touch your flirting interest. If you sense any tension or zero reciprocation, back off.

Wait for the Green Light

Before you decide to use a flirtatious touch, look for the following signs. Notice when:

- He moves closer to you
- She blocks out the rest of the world to listen to you

- He leans over to tell you something in your ear or at close range
- She places her hands close enough to touch yours
- He touches you

A Touching Review for Women

Once you get the go-ahead-and-touch vibe, be bold and sneak a touch! Be spontaneous and stay in the moment. Any of the following will put a smile on his face.

- Touching his hand, wrist, arm, or shoulder
- Admiring and touching his ring or watch
- Giving him a light, playful push
- Removing a piece of string or lint from his sweater or jacket

Are you a bit shy about extending the first touch? Try "accidentally" touching him first. Here are a few ways that have the best results:

- When handing him anything, let your fingers linger next to his for a few milliseconds.
- When walking next to him, let your hand brush against his.
- When he reaches for something, "accidentally" move your hands in his direction so your hands touch.
- When seated next to each other, let your legs touch momentarily.

People may hear your words, but they feel your attitude.

JOHN C. MAXWELL

A Touching Review for Men

Guys, when you're flirtatiously touching a woman, less is more. Any of the following touches will let her know you are interested.

- Touching her hand, arm, wrist, or shoulder
- Placing your hand on her lower back to give her the right of way
- Complimenting her and quickly touching her watch, bracelet, or ring
- Brushing against her "accidentally" and watching her reaction
- Gently grasping her hand and admiring her nails or hands
- While walking, holding her hand for a few seconds and then letting it go
- When seated next to each other, letting your foot or leg briefly touch her foot or leg

If there's a smile, a relaxed acceptance of your touch, or reciprocation, you've hit the jackpot. Those are sure signs she likes you. Remember, though, this doesn't give you the green light to keep touching.

If you get a startled reaction to your touch, offer an apology, such as, "So very sorry if I offended you." Try making your flirting interest comfortable again with a fun, lighthearted conversation. Also, don't take it personally: She simply may not have been expecting the touch. Sometimes, recoiling at something surprising is an involuntary reaction.

MIRRORING DEMONSTRATES INTEREST

Mirroring is one of flirting's best-kept secrets. Mirroring means we tend to mimic the behaviors of people we are attracted to. Conversely, if the cues are not (noticed or) reciprocated, chances are, your flirting interest has his attention elsewhere.

What is mirroring? It's mimicking whatever your flirting interest does–subtly. Emulate your crush's body language, voice volume and tone, gestures and movements. You reflect back what she does and the other person instantly feels more comfortable around you. Congratulations, you've sparked a connection through body language alone! Mirroring is always understated, but there's nothing subtle about its results. Read on and I'll tell you all about it.

WHY MIRROR?

Mirroring creates an instant bond between flirters. Imagine you're with your flirting interest–let's call her Tracy. As you lean in toward her, she ever so slightly moves a bit closer. A few minutes later, because the music is really loud, you speak into Tracy's ear so she can hear you. A minute later, she motions you to come closer; she wants to tell you something. How do you feel? Could this one be a keeper? This is marvelous mirroring in motion!

Basically, mirroring is flattery. You demonstrate to the other person that you are in tune with them. Instinctively, we gravitate toward those who behave similarly to us. Therefore, when you naturally mirror your flirting interest, you send out a flare that says you feel an attraction. So, if your flirting interest jokes, your mirroring action is to joke back. If he moves to the music, sway to the music as well.

With the right body language, it's easy to flirt without saying a word. And in chapter 3, which is all about digital flirting, you'll learn how to convey "body language" over text–using your own unique style to match your emotions and your personality.

Mirroring in Action

Lisa and Pete met at happy hour one Friday afternoon. Pete was sitting at the bar and Lisa walked in with a cane. Pete asked her whether she'd like to sit down and she accepted. At first, Lisa wasn't sure whether Pete really wanted her there or whether he was simply being polite. They began chatting, and next thing she knew it was an hour later. In our coaching session, Lisa mentioned that when she touched Pete's arm, he reciprocated. When she adjusted her chair, he adjusted his. "It was as if he was saying, 'I really like you,'" Lisa said. "I had no idea then that mirroring was happening. It just felt that we were on the same page."

Where am I going to meet an architect who lives in Brooklyn besides Tinder at this point? I like it, it's fun, *it's the modern-day singles bar.*

ANDY COHEN

CHAPTER 3

The Fine Art of Digital Flirting

EXUDE CONFIDENCE AND BRING ROMANCE INTO YOUR LIFE

Every loving relationship starts with a smile, a wink, or an opening line, regardless of the way you meet.

Flirting electronically can feel overwhelming for some; for others, flirting with a screen as a barrier is a huge relief. Still, flirting without a warm body right in front of you can be a bit nerve-racking: You have to wait for a response, after all. Even swiping right is enough to give you butterflies!

Regardless of your comfort level, flirtatious exchanges online are the norm in today's world of social media, dating apps, and dating websites. Digital flirting opens up new ways to pursue romance. Consider yourself lucky to have so many choices!

WELCOME TO TWENTY-FIRST CENTURY FLIRTING!

I'm here to show you how you can maximize your success on social media, dating sites, and apps, even if you've resisted embracing the technology because it feels overwhelming. But here's where knowledge is power! If you feel you're in the dark about flirting digitally, your natural response is to avoid it. Try thinking about it differently: What about all the possible matches (and dates!) that are just a click, like, or text away? Keep reminding yourself of that to stay motivated and driven. It's all about your attitude, so let's readjust: It's time to get excited about all your potential flirting options. And I'll calm your nerves by giving you the knowledge, skills, and tips you need to be the best digital flirt out there.

Start with the platform that interests you the most or seems the easiest to master, or the one you think "everyone but you" is having success with! After that, you can move on to the platforms that seem a bit more challenging. Don't wait: Procrastination breeds self-doubt and worry, so the quicker you get moving on this, the easier it will be to implement your enticing, engaging flirting strategies.

Don't worry if you feel ambivalent, experience sensory overload, or are confused by the lingo (friending, follow, tweet/retweet, gif, direct message ([DM], etc.). This chapter fills you in on everything you need to know—and will ease your anxiety—about flirting on Instagram, Facebook, Twitter, online dating sites and apps, and when texting. I describe all your options in detail, so you'll have the expertise and confidence to use the wide array of digital choices available, and I'll even show you how you can flirt without joining a single dating site or app. (Really!) Plus, I'll help you become a better digital flirt by introducing you to the secret rules of online, texting, and social media flirting etiquette. I'll give you specific examples of what you can say in your messages, and show you how flirting electronically will increase your dating possibilities. I'll also show you how to make digital flirting a fun, exciting adventure.

That said, just like flirting face-to-face, there will be times when you'll feel discouraged, confused, or wish connecting with someone was easier. If those feelings bubble up, it's okay to take a digital time-out. Taking a break is a good thing: It gives you time to refresh your enthusiasm and motivation—even if it seems to have disappeared temporarily. Don't worry: It happens to everyone.

I urge you to try all the options, because you never know which one will work best for you until you try it. You might think some of these possibilities aren't for you, but try them anyway. The ones that seem least appealing just might end up being the most fun—and the ones that yield the best results!

TEXTING

Texting is the most universal way to flirt, and the flirting possibilities of texting are limitless! Texting allows you to craft your best flirt without distractions and without the anticipation of seeing an instantaneous reaction. When you're flirting over text, you can add, delete, and even get a friend's opinion if you need another set of eyes—all before you hit send. Those are all advantages, but, still, it's fine to be spontaneous and not overthink your words, too! Having fun with it is the most important thing.

Here's why: A flirty text is about setting the mood and creating a funny, warm, playful, teasing vibe between you and your crush. Your aim is to put a smile on your crush's face by being charming and even a bit gutsy. Sharing only facts (baseball scores, weather prediction, latest news) does not create a warm, intimate, romantic feeling. If you do talk about something factual (work, holidays, hobbies), try to relate it in some way to the relationship between you and your flirting interest. For instance, you might say, "I made three goals in hockey last night. If only you could have been there to see it, because it will never happen again (lol)." Or, "I had such a stressful day today, texting you is the best part of my day." And this one is sure to melt your crush's heart: "I just found myself thinking about you for no apparent reason and it felt good."

Today was my lucky day!

I'm so glad I met you.

Aww! That's so nice!

Ditto for me ♥

HOW TO BE A TEXTING FLIRT

Here's a quick review of the basics: Be complimentary, have fun, ask unpredictable questions, demonstrate empathy, and show off who you are. It's perfectly okay to strut your stuff (passions, accomplishments, dreams, even embarrassing moments)—in fact, it's highly recommended! But there are times when words alone are not enough to convey your flirtatious nonverbal message. You want your personality to shine through and keep the flirt going. Sometimes, you just have to think outside the (text) box, brighten the lights, and turn up the volume to get your flirt across! Here are three ways to do just that:

Emojis. The word "emoji" comes from the Japanese words *picture* (*E*) and *character* (*moji*), and emojis are symbols that express your emotions and your body language. They are designed as a modern shorthand to convey a feeling: For instance, ☺ is a universal symbol for being happy. Emojis are a quick and easy way to spice up your text. They give it a soft touch with small clever images that reflect facial expressions or feelings,

activities, food and drink, travel or locations, objects, animals, and nature. Many devices have built-in emoji keyboards.

Emojis can mirror your body language, mood, and feelings when words fall short. I'm a big fan of the red heart, smiley face, wink, and thumbs-up. They can be fun and flirty—just don't overuse them.

Your personal avatar. For an imaginative way to express your feelings and thoughts, create a "lifelike" cartoon avatar of yourself. Mine is a fit, blonde, smiling gal. Once created, you can choose from a variety of topics and feelings, such as getting together, thanks, birthdays, sports, or thinking of you. All you have to do is download a personal emoji app, such as Bitmoji. You can also add a few of your own words to give your emoji a personal touch. If you find yourself struggling with how to say, "I'm thinking of you," Bitmoji has one that says, "Got You on My Mind." It's s a gutsy-yet-warm way of getting your message across.

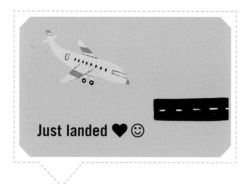

Just landed ♥ ☺

So, instead of texting, "I'm home from my trip," send an emoji with your personal avatar that says, "Just landed." Or, thank the person who changed your flat tire by sending "You Are a Life Saver." Another great one is the picture of the person cleaning, cooking, talking on the phone, and having a cup of coffee at the same time. It's a great way to say, "I know you are juggling so many things." It's clever, very playful, and sure to get you noticed!

GIFs Rock. A GIF is a video snippet, often from pop culture (television, film, or music). "GIF" stands for "graphics interchange format," and its correct pronunciation is hotly debated, but it varies between "GIF" with a hard *g* and "JIF" with a soft *j* sound. It's an attention-getter that can communicate your feelings and thoughts in a way that just pops! It's as if you are sending your crush a virtual bouquet, a special greeting

card, or an image that perfectly describes your feelings. It adds a playful quality to your text, which, as you know, is a flirting must. GIFs are commonly available via apps or widgets you can download on your phone. You can search for and find GIFs related to almost any topic or feeling. They liven things up, create a feeling of connection and intimacy, and set the mood—something that a words-only text can't achieve. I love the GIF of the kid going from sitting to sleeping on the couch in a nanosecond (a great way to say, "I'm exhausted"). Or the cat who continually shakes his head "no" (ideal when you want to say no in a very lighthearted, even hilarious, way), or the baby grinning from ear to ear while pointing her finger at you as if she's telling you you're funny and naughty! (That's the perfect GIF to use when you want to respond to something funny and sexy your crush just said.)

Some say the best part of using GIFs is that it takes the pressure off you to come up with the perfect words and sentiments—GIFs do it for you. Here are a few keywords to choose from: smile, thanks, miss you, wink, embarrassed, hugs, laughter.

THE TWELVE MOST IMPORTANT DOS AND DON'TS OF TEXTING

A good flirty text conversation is more than just checking in, asking a question, or sending a heart or a wink. If you want your texts to soar to new flirting heights, read on!

✔ **Definitely** flash your fun side, make jokes, be playful. Having a sense of humor and not taking yourself too seriously are incredibly sexy!

✘ **Don't** end every text with ha-ha, lol, or hehe. Overkill is deadly, and doesn't add anything to your message. In fact, it actually detracts from the possibility of being cute and cool.

✔ **Definitely** send photos that mirror your message. They will enhance and complement your message. A tasteful yet sexy pic is certainly okay.

✘ **Don't** send lewd or birthday suit shots, especially unsolicited ones. Receiving nude photos can be a deal breaker as well as a big turn-off.

Worse, they can easily be shown to others or posted online, which could have negative consequences. Even if someone you like requests one, save it until you've built up a trusting relationship. Sending nude photos gives the impression that a hookup is the only thing on your mind: If that's not the meaning you intended, it'll be tough to get the conversation back to getting to know each other.

✔ **Definitely** think of texting as a face-to-face conversation. Limit your text to a few sentences at most, then await your crush's response. It's a lot like a great tennis match: There should be lots of back and forth.

✘ **Don't** send multiple texts before you get an answer. That's exactly like calling someone five times with no call back. Take the hint!

✔ **Definitely** compliment, ask questions, or display that you care. It's the best way to show sincere interest.

✘ **Don't** just say "Hi," "Hey," or "Sup." Using those words alone is a sure way to end the flirt because your crush will not feel special or valued. They may actually make your crush wonder whether you're really into them, since you might come across as lazy or indifferent, or as if you just want to "check in" with minimal effort. The receiver of the text might also feel uneasy and unsure of how to respond, because you haven't offered anything specific to respond to.

✔ **Definitely** text to express your feelings. Text after a date to say you had a great time and want to continue the conversation; text for no reason other than to keep the flirt going; text because it feels right. Being spontaneous and thoughtful is so flattering!

✘ **Don't** be stingy or blasé when it comes to expressing how you feel. Your flirting interest can't read your mind.

✔ **Definitely** project the best (real) you. Honesty is always the best policy, and it's the only way to flirt.

✘ **Don't** pretend to be someone you're not (you say you're a college grad, but you only took one semester of freshman math), lie about your likes and dislikes (you say you love cats, but are allergic and can't stand them), or stretch the truth about the facts (your age, your job, your marital status). No one likes to be lied to, and the only person you end up disappointing is yourself.

✔ **Definitely** pay attention to grammar and spelling.

✘ **Don't** rely on texting shorthand. If your text is difficult to decipher, your crush may feel confused or even irritated. If you're not going to take the time to write out a text in full, you give the impression you prefer to take shortcuts—and that's not always a good thing.

✔ **Definitely** use emojis and use punctuation appropriately. They are intended to express your feelings without using words, and can also be used to enhance your words. Well-placed emojis and punctuation add interest and excitement to your text, and using them also shows you took time to search for the perfect emoji to reflect your feelings to your crush.

✖ **Don't** overuse emojis, GIFs, or punctuation. Your love interest might think you can't put a sentence together; your message may be misinterpreted; or your crush might find all those exclamation points irritating.

✔ **Definitely** vary your texts to keep your flirting fresh. Send a personal emoji text today, a GIF tomorrow, a GIF with words the next day, and a words-only text the day after that.

✖ **Don't** send a barrage of GIFs, personal emojis, or emoticons. It just kills the mood and detracts from your flirty intentions. Your intended will hit delete immediately!

Secret Rule Revealed: The Ultimate Texting Turnoffs

Because so much flirting takes place via text these days, it's vital that you woo your flirting interest, not make him or her cringe. And it's not just about the content of your text: It's *how* you convey your words on the screen that makes all the difference. Following are the results of a study conducted by students at Stanford University of 1,000 adults and young people:

The biggest turn-offs for both sexes are:

- Very informal spelling
- Lack of grammar and punctuation
- Overuse of slang
- All lowercase letters

So, take the time to proofread your texts. It shows your crush you care.

✔ **Definitely** be a classy texter. Think before you text! The classiest texters have a sense of humor, are concise, polite, and only say in text what they would say in person. They are always mindful of how the text will be received.

✘ **Don't** sext or send a text when you are drunk! Once you press send, you can NEVER take back what you texted. Besides, flirting should not be a sexual or a drunken come-on.

✔ **Definitely** be mindful of texting someone during the workday. If you do, just send a few words to show you're thinking of him.

✘ **Don't** send texts when you know it will be disturbing, distracting, or if it can wait until your crush is "off duty."

✔ **Definitely** text your crush when you know she is awake. Your thoughtfulness will be appreciated, and it suggests you want to be a part of your crush's daily life. She will know she is on your mind if you text when she's waking up (which shows you know when her workday begins) or in the later part of evening (which shows you know what time she usually goes to bed). It's a perfect way to put a smile on her face.

✘ **Don't** text your crush during sleeping hours. It's a turn-off, because the spontaneity and back-and-forth banter isn't possible, and it'll look like your crush isn't on your mind during waking hours!

BEWARE OF THE SERIAL TEXTER

I'm about to save you a ton of time (you can thank me later): Don't be fooled by the perpetual texter! This is the person you meet online or in person, and you really hit it off with. The texts are flirty, and you're saying to yourself, *I think I finally met a good one!* You may get texts several times a day, or once a week, or off and on for a month or two, but they never include a plan to get together. They make you feel special one minute, and so sure that a date is going to happen—and then, radio silence.

But, eventually, the texter resurfaces. This annoying—and misleading—habit is known as "breadcrumbing."

Don't settle for a breadcrumber! Here's what to do if you think you might be flirting with one. If you are exchanging flirty texts for a few days and no date is on the horizon, say, "Let's make a plan to get together this weekend," or "I'd love to try that new burger place. How's Wednesday for you?" If the response is noncommittal or sounds something like, "That sounds good, I'll let you know when my schedule is less hectic," here's what you should say: "I'm interested in seeing if we have chemistry in person, so, with that said, I'd love to meet in person. Text me when you want to get together." That way you leave the door open, but don't waste your time having a pseudo love affair via text!

INSTAGRAM

Not everyone knows it, but flirting possibilities do exist on Instagram! Since photos are the lifeblood of Instagram, they give you so much to comment on. However, because Instagram is not a dating site, your flirting moves should reflect what you would do in person. The goal is always to have fun, be playful, and make the other person feel terrific.

Insta-Flirt

Instagram is the social media app of the future. The younger generation is flocking to Instagram just like Generation X flocked to Facebook. With 500 million daily users, 40 billion photos shared, and 4.2 billion likes per day, Instagram is abuzz with interesting people. You never know where your follow may take you!

YOUR PROFILE

Make sure your profile is public (not private) so everyone can view your profile and follow you. Making your profile private means you're unapproachable: You're using "virtual body language" that pushes people away! Your photo should be your best head shot (make sure you are easily recognizable, just in case someone is checking you out). You only have 150 characters for your bio, so make sure you include the fact that you're single, who you are, what you do, and give your followers a glimpse of your personality so they have a reason to follow you. For example, "pharmacist by day, fine wine lover and staying fit by night, single dad of twins, with time to find love. #merlot #cycling #divorced #WashingtonDC #RollingStones."

FOLLOW TO FLIRT

Following someone is a low-risk way to test the flirtatious waters. You will get their attention because most of us check out who is following us. First, follow her, or request to follow her if she has a private profile, and then wait a day or two before you click on the heart to like a recent post. Too many likes too often scream "obsessive" and you don't want to come across as creepy or stalker-ish.

You can follow someone who catches your eye or you can search for hashtags of people with similar interests, like #gokarts, #vegan, or #italy. Once you do that, you can follow a variety of people with similar interests. If someone follows you back, that's a great sign—even better if he likes your posts! And if he comments on your photo, you've hit the jackpot.

If someone has a private profile and doesn't accept your request, view it the same way you would if you approached someone in a bar and she wasn't interested in you. If that happened, you'd simply move on, right? It's the same with Instagram.

TURN ON POST NOTIFICATIONS

Do you want to know every time your crush posts something? Instagram has the "turn on post notifications" feature (which you can switch on). This notifies you every time he posts something. That way, you don't have to check all day long. Whew, what a relief!

LIKES AND COMMENTS

How often should you like/comment on your flirting interest's posts? I suggest no more than once or twice a week—unless you come across a post that gives you a perfect flirting opportunity you simply cannot pass by. Make sure you "like" an assortment of your crush's photos—like a selfie today, a quote tomorrow, and a picture with friends another day. Be sure not to like every post: It comes across as overkill. When it comes to liking posts, less is more unless your crush posts only once or twice a month. You might want to see whether she has another social media account she is more active on.

DIRECT MESSAGE

You can send a direct (private) message (DM) on Instagram to your crush. If you don't know the person, be engaging and present your best self in the same way you would approach a prospective professional connection for an in-person meeting. You can also include a photo from your camera roll. This is the time to be clear about your intention to meet.

The golden rule of Instagram flirting is, don't be creepy and annoying! If you send one or two DMs and get no response, take the hint. You'll never know why your crush didn't respond, so don't waste your time wondering about it. (FYI, Instagram lets you know if your message has been read: It displays the word "seen" once the recipient reads it.)

POST AN INSTAGRAM STORY

An Instagram story is a temporary video or picture(s) that disappears twenty-four hours after its posting time. Here's how it works: Let's say a friend posts an Instagram story and you spot someone that piques your interest. If that person is tagged, i.e., @lovebugfran, lucky you: Just click on her handle and it will bring you to her profile page. You can follow her, make a comment, like a photo, and some even have an email option. The mutual friend you share makes for a great flirting segue! Make sure you mention that you both know "Jaime" and see where it takes you.

TAP ON THE SNAPSHOT THAT CATCHES YOUR EYE

You are scrolling through your feed and you see a cutie on a feed that you follow. Tap once lightly on that person. If a person icon appears, it means he was tagged. Click on the person's Instagram handle, which will take you to his profile. Once you are there, your options are to DM, like a photo, or make a flirty comment. Be careful not to accidentally double-tap a photo—this will "like" the photo—unless it's your intention to do that.

TAKE ADVANTAGE OF SECOND CHANCES

Let's say you were at a bar and spotted someone you wanted to talk to, but never did. You can search on Instagram for the bar (i.e., Temple Bar in Dublin) and see if you can spot her in a recent post. If you know the person who posted the photo, ask for an introduction. If she is tagged in the photo, you can get her Instagram handle, and you can send a flirty DM. You can also make a comment on a post—perhaps she will follow you.

PERFECT YOUR SNOOPING SKILLS

If you want to check out the attendees of a local chapter of an organization or community program, go to Instagram and take a look at their posts. You'll get a chance to see who the attendees are, and when you attend the next meeting you'll have things to talk about because you have "virtually" been there.

TOP HASHTAG TIPS

Definitely use hashtags. Anyone searching for a hashtag you used will be able to view your Instagram account if it is public—and that equals more flirting opportunities. Sprinkle in one or two of the top ten to get the most engagement.

Stick to a max of eight hashtags, according to Scot Ayres, coauthor of *Facebook All-in-One for Dummies*. There are diverse opinions on the ideal number of hashtags: Social Fresh suggests using seven, while Track Maven suggests eleven. Although Instagram allows you to use thirty hashtags, too many can make you appear desperate and self-centered. Excessive use of hashtags in social media is equivalent to the person who never knows when to stop talking—and most of us know what it's like to be on the receiving end of a nonstop talker. It makes you want to run for the hills.

Use hashtags related to your photo. Here's a great takeaway from

TOP TEN HASHTAGS

#love
#instagood
#me
#tbt
#cute
#photooftheday
#instamood
#beautiful
#picoftheday
#igers

(Webstagram)

businesses that use Instagram: They use hashtags to create brand recognition and represent themselves in the most meaningful way. You want to do the same by using hashtags that reflect who you are and what you stand for. Hashtags are a sensational way to market yourself in clever and unique ways.

GET NOTICED WITH FACEBOOK FLIRTING

Facebook is another gem in your digital flirting crown. It's free, fun, and the numbers are staggering: As of 2017, there are more than one billion mobile daily active users. And it can lead to meeting someone with whom you might never have connected.

Although Facebook is not a dating site, you can use it as a platform to flirt with "friends," "friends of friends," and "potential new friends." Flirting with your virtual friends is just that: being friendly, fun loving, and conversational.

In May 2018, Facebook announced plans to launch a dating app designed to build long-term relationships—not just hookups.

In the announcement, Mark Zuckerberg, CEO of Facebook, explained that the optional feature will create a dating profile entirely separate from your original profile—in fact, your Facebook friends won't even see your dating profile and it won't show up in your news feed. Users will also be able to find local events and message people planning to attend. If a potential match responds, you can connect via a brand-new text messaging feature.

Until the app officially launches, here's how to maximize your flirting opportunities on Facebook.

Profile. Your profile is your online face. It gives people a snapshot of who you are (your personality, interests, occupation, and passions). Make sure to include your relationship status as single. There is no reason to keep it a secret—being single isn't a fatal disease! Make it clear that you are single and happy, not thirsty or desperate for a love interest. Also, remember that your Facebook profile is your personal brand, so make it active and vibrant. Post your favorite photos—ones that make your personality and looks come alive. Ditch the bare-chested, scantily clad pics and the barrage of selfies. View your profile as your "personal digital wingperson:" First impressions are vital; you want your profile to be approachable, appealing, and to offer your flirting interests lots to comment on and inquire about. Make sure your privacy settings are set to public so everyone can see who you are and what you post, and can send you a friend request or private message.

Your Wall. What's the gold standard for your posts? Vary them, post photos of friends and family, pictures of you alone, videos, vacation posts, activities you enjoy, quotes, or something you are passionate about. Intriguing, funny, or heartwarming comments make your posts come alive and encourage others to comment. (Post comments or photos you would only share in face-to-face interactions.) Lastly, post regularly: I suggest one to three posts a week. Excessive posting can irritate your friends and it will likely cause them to glaze over when they see your posts because they know a gazillion more are in the works.

Flirting on Someone Else's Wall. Your Facebook flirting should emulate flirting in real life, that is, it should be authentic. If you want to show your crush you are interested, like his current posts—in moderation, and not just the macho or sexy ones. Commenting on her posts is the equivalent of using your best opening lines. If he posts about movies or music, share your tastes, too. If she asks for advice or has a question, offer to help. If someone is looking for a top-notch car mechanic, tell him you have the best car mechanic that you are willing to share—but only with him! Add something like "good mechanics aren't expensive; they're priceless!" Remember, whatever you post is visible to everyone, so be sure that whatever you say on Facebook is something you would also say in person.

Friends of Friends. You spot someone who is a friend of a friend and you are interested in getting to know the person. Luckily, you have your virtual wingperson at your disposal. Message your friend and say

> "
>
> The worst thing you can do is nothing.
>
> **THEODORE ROOSEVELT**

something like this: "I saw this woman on your wall, the one who was (at the book launch/getting the award at the fund-raiser for Crohn's disease/standing next to you at the housewarming party). She really impressed me and I'd like to meet her. Do you know if she is available? If so, could you let her know that I'm interested and pave the way for me? I would so appreciate it. If she's not interested, that's okay, too."

Couple's Photos. Make sure to delete photos of you and your ex if you want to be flirted with! If you don't want to get rid of them forever, just change the privacy settings of your albums and photos to "only me." If the photo was posted by someone else, you can't delete it, but you can remove your tag and it will be removed from your timeline. Your photos are your flirting props, so include ones that will spark interest and mystery and give people lots to comment on.

Create an Event. Posting an event on Facebook is a cool way to expand your social network and practice your flirting skills at the event you organize. Being the host gives you a huge advantage: Your job is to meet and greet everyone. (I just love how the digital world gives you an incentive to have fun in person!) You can organize a "Flirty Friday" at your favorite restaurant, bar, bookstore café, or anywhere you'd like. Plan a Sunday brunch, beach volleyball and barbeque, volunteer gig, Singles' Awareness Day gathering, Friendsgiving, Valentine's Day party for singles, or a free concert. Posting your event on Facebook is an effective and efficient way to spread the word: You can ask your friends to share it, and they can post it on groups they belong to. You can also request an RSVP.

Facebook Messaging. This enables you to be flirtatious with someone you know, or with a perfect stranger, because you are sending a private message (PM). It's a great option because only you and your crush can see it. If you don't know the person but have a friend in common, make sure to mention the connection: It makes for an intriguing, reliable introduction. Let her know what inspired you to connect and that you'd love to meet in person for a drink or coffee—something quick and casual.

Four Rules to Get You Noticed on Facebook

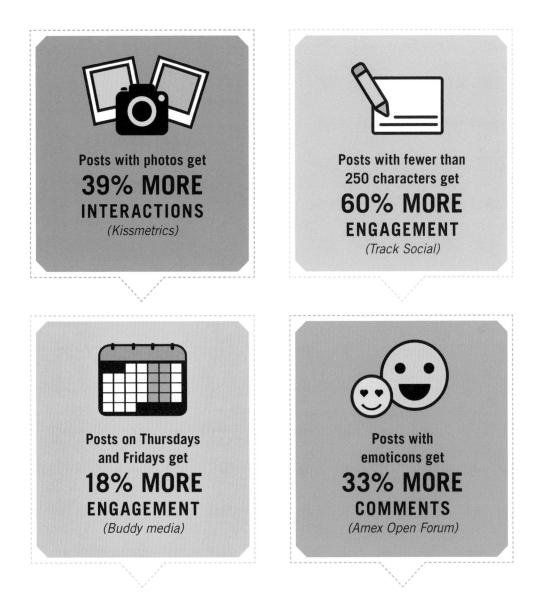

Posts with photos get
39% MORE
INTERACTIONS
(Kissmetrics)

Posts with fewer than
250 characters get
60% MORE
ENGAGEMENT
(Track Social)

Posts on Thursdays
and Fridays get
18% MORE
ENGAGEMENT
(Buddy media)

Posts with
emoticons get
33% MORE
COMMENTS
(Amex Open Forum)

If you stumble across someone who fascinates you and you can't stop thinking about how much you'd like to meet him, you can be super brave and send a PM. Be friendly, complimentary, and honest. Say something like this, "Carlos, I'm Fran, and I was drawn to your profile because of your love of kayaking and your great smile. I did it once and loved it but I had no sense of steering and had to be hauled in to shore by a fellow kayaker. If you'd like to meet for a cup of coffee to talk about how I could perfect my kayaking, let me know. If not, or if you are taken, I understand. Thanks ☺."

ONLINE FLIRTING IS THE KEY TO FINDING LOVE

You've signed up for an online dating site or app—finally! Now what? Sit back and wait for your virtual soulmate to find you, or be as flirty and proactive as you possibly can? (Guess which is the right answer?) It's time to take the initiative and get your flirt on!

The challenge of flirting online is making a connection and creating interest and chemistry without the face-to-face contact. Although it can be challenging, once you master the art of online flirting, it will become second nature to you.

Let's do a three-second review of how to flirt in person: Be playful, have fun, show your vulnerability, smile, make eye contact, exude confidence, ask questions, compliment, and look your best. Sounds familiar, right? Now I'll show you how to translate real-life flirting into flirting onscreen with your virtual match. Let's begin with your initial message. Its purpose is to ignite interest, show you feel comfortable in your own skin, and quickly transition you from being a stranger to being someone your crush wants to meet (and vice versa, of course). Without the visual cues, it will take some creativity and ingenuity to make your flirting come alive on the screen. Here's how to do just that.

SIX WAYS TO BE AN INCREDIBLE ONLINE FLIRT

1 Just like you, your words should look their best.

Here's your chance to make a sensational first impression. Your message will either entice your flirting interest to read on or to hit delete. What can you do to keep the flirt alive? Use spell-check, please! One or two typos are no big deal, but a message filled with spelling errors is a virtual turn-off. It's equivalent to showing complete disinterest in real life. I know your time is precious, but if your message takes too much time for your match to decode, it can be a deal breaker. Never write something like this: "*Hey, whtsup? How ru doin. tnite? It wood be gr8 if unI cood tawk asap. Thx TTYL.*"

Your punctuation conveys your sense of humor, your facial expressions—even your vocal inflections. For instance, if dancing is your passion, place an exclamation mark at the end of the sentence. Or if you love convertibles, type LOVE in all caps. This way you make your excitement jump off the page. Sprinkle in an emoticon: It's the equivalent of eye contact and a smile in real life.

1 OUT OF 3 MARRIAGES STARTS ONLINE

According to a study published in *Proceedings of the National Academy of Sciences*, approximately one out of three marriages starts with an online message. That's great news!

Try a wink, a smile, or a smile with a heart—all soften and warm your message. I love ellipses (. . .) because they are mysterious and imply you have some juicy info you are holding back until you connect another time. Very enticing! You might say, "I was out for my morning walk and then, out of nowhere, I tripped and . . . I'll give you the details another time. You won't believe what happened." Parentheses are a good way to add meaningful asides to your messages. "The jewelry you design is so unique (Wow! you are so talented) and really stunning."

2 Open with playfulness and humor.

Your first sentence is your opening line. Think of it as your online version of eye contact, a smile, and inviting body language. If you start with an amusing question or comment, you will get the virtual conversation started (she will be answering you in her own mind)

Here are a few opening lines to get you thinking. I know they are a bit outrageous, but sometimes you just have to push the envelope! Adapt them to your personal style.

- "I typed and erased my opening line to you three times. Just in case you're wondering why, I think you are a "mensch" (good guy) and cute as well. So, now I can relax and be myself."

- "I love your sense of humor and hope you might chuckle at the only joke I know: What did the little firecracker say to the big fire-cracker? . . . What's up, Pop?"

- "Just curious: What kitchen utensil would best describe you? Just wondering if anyone has ever asked you that? I'm hoping not, so I could be your first. ☺"

- Ask a seasonal question like, "What's your favorite Halloween candy? Mine is . . ."

- "Which could you most easily live without—your phone for two days, internet for two days, or Netflix for two weeks?"

- "If I could bring you your favorite guilty-pleasure foods, what would they be? (Please, no more than 10) lol"

3 No novels, please.

The first message you send should be between 75 and 200 words. Remember, the purpose of your initial message is to stimulate interest so your match writes back. A long, wordy story is boring: Your match won't read it, so don't waste your time. Instead, write a quick note to let him know that, out of all the possibilities, you picked him! That is always your goal. (BTW: That paragraph is only 67 words.)

4 Be conversational.

Make sure you type like you talk, and imagine you're talking to your flirting interest in person. For example, you might say, "I'm a nurse and I enjoy helping people." That's nice, but stiff and a bit boring. If you met in person and you started talking about your job, you'd probably say, "I'm an ER nurse: My adrenaline kicks in the minute I hear the ambulance arrive and I get the alert as to what to expect. Sometimes, it's life or death, and other times, I just have to reassure the patient that all will be fine." Or, if you want to talk about foods you like, "My favorite foods are Italian, sushi, and burgers," sounds like you are reading from a script. I want your words to come alive so the other person can see, smell, taste, and feel your words. Try rephrasing it this way: "If you promise not to tell anyone, I'll confess that I love fast-food burgers

and fries (even though I try not to have them too often). I have never met a pizza I didn't love, and the chill of fresh sushi with a hint of ginger on my palate is my all-time favorite."

I know it's hard, but imagine that the person you are writing to is someone who likes you, someone you feel at ease with, and someone whom you want to impress with being yourself. When you visualize it in this way, it becomes so much easier to be chatty and natural.

5 Dish out compliments.

Compliments have universal appeal. It feels terrific to be noticed, appreciated, and valued, and self-doubt melts away the moment you receive a compliment. It's the number-one way to make your flirting interest feel special. Read his profile, view all her photos, and take note of anything that puts a smile on your face or something that you think is special. It's the best way to start a conversation, both in person and online. The best compliments are honest and have an element of surprise: The more specific and out of the ordinary, the greater the impact. For example, "The kindness you demonstrate to the boy you tutor is very touching." "I had such fun reading the story about how you couldn't find your white rental car in Disneyworld (you turned a nightmare into something hilarious. PS: Just wait until I tell you my missing car story . . .)" "I love your dimples." "You have the nicest shoes." "You are adorable and you're always smiling–what a great combination."

6 Close with intrigue.

There's a lot of competition when it comes to online dating, so you want to do everything in your power to encourage your match to want to meet you in person. So, end your message with something that will inspire your match to respond to you. You want your match to feel that she is the only person on the dating site or app you want to meet. Here are some captivating closings:

- "I hope you want to meet me as much as I want to meet you. I almost didn't go on the site tonight, but I'm glad that I did!"

- "I'd love to meet you."

- "The best way to find out if we are the perfect match is to meet for a cup of coffee: Your shop or mine?"

- "How funny that we both hate blue cheese and cauliflower! Let's meet and discover what else we have in common."

- "Do you believe in *bashert* (it's meant to be)? Maybe that will be us. Let's meet and see, you just never know!"

- "Thanks for posting your profile; it inspired me to message you. I got such a good feeling about you."

- "I found myself nodding in agreement with everything you wrote and your photos were the icing on the cake!"Maybe today is our lucky day!"

- "Look forward to meeting you sooner rather than later."

TWITTER

Flirting on Twitter is the "golden mean" of a chance meeting and a swipe right! And it's the next generation of speed dating. (Plus, you now have 280 characters to get noticed or send a flirty tweet!) Twitter is a public social-networking site, not a dating app, but it has been trending as a low-risk platform for flirting. Perhaps you went to a friend's graduation party, attended a happy hour, met someone at a seminar, or talked to someone at a concert, and all you know is a name and maybe some basic information. Why not turn to Twitter to flirt with your crush? Give her a random compliment, laugh at his jokes, or send kudos for an accomplishment or a good deed.

New to Twitter? No problem. Here are the basics:

Create an eye-catching profile. Choose a Twitter avatar you are proud of. It could be a fabulous photo of yourself or an eye-catching avatar that's a real-life image of you. Compose an attention-grabbing bio, that is, one that expresses who you are and what you want. For example, "Eternal Optimist, wanting to spend the rest of my life loving my soulmate, designing buildings, and always having time to make someone's life better. How about you?"

> Stop being afraid of what could go wrong and start being excited about what could be right.
>
> **AUTHOR UNKNOWN**

Follow strategically. Meg loves music, so she follows artists, DJs, and electronic music lovers. So, she started following Jake and they tweeted about all things music related. And then he sent her a direct message (DM) and invited her to go to a local music festival. She said yes, and had a great time. He asked if she would go to dinner with him the next day. She said sure, and they exchanged phone numbers.

Follow people with similar interests or careers. Choose your favorite authors or celebrities, or even those who are newly single. When someone follows you, it's the equivalent of saying hi. In real life you'd say hi back, so go ahead and follow them back on Twitter—unless they give you a creepy feeling!

Interact with your crush. If your crush tweets something, answer with a flirty reply. "Wow, you took the words right out of my mouth." "You have such passion for . . ." "If only I could have come up with that comment." If you really want to make an impression, retweet or "like" what he said: It's the equivalent of an in-person compliment. Tweet funny, witty, interesting things. It gives your crush something to comment on. Here are some words of caution, though: Flirt with one person at a time, and if you don't want your boss, customers, or family reading your tweets, don't hit "Tweet." On that note, it's time to move on to direct messaging.

Don't be shy: Send a direct message. Direct messaging allows you to flirt privately, with the added bonus of being able to use more than 280 characters. You can send a direct message to your crush and only she will see it. It's the modern way of saying, "It's so noisy in here. Why don't you move a bit closer?" It's the perfect way to figure out whether the two of you want to move the relationship from Twitter to real life. That means it's the time and the place to share your phone numbers.

CONGRATULATIONS!

At the end of your digital-flirting day, take the gamble, and meet with your crush face-to-face. You will be so glad you took the chance. If you get a thumbs-up, exchange cell phone numbers and make a plan. Always remember to meet in a public place, get to the date and home on your own, and have a charged cell phone with you. If it's a match, YEAH! If not, better you know sooner rather than later so you can wink at someone new–the digital inventory of possible matches is constantly replenished and updated.

You are resilient, confident, and quite a savvy digital flirt. The more platforms you engage in, the more fun you'll have, and flirting online will always feel fresh and invigorating.

And, the more at ease you are, the more you'll want to flirt–both on and off screen. Remember: The best day of your life could be when you swipe right!

In the next chapter, you'll learn how to break the ice and strike up a conversation in person with just about anyone.

"

If you don't go after what you want, *you'll never have it.*

If you don't ask, *the answer is always no.*

If you don't step forward, you're *always in the same place.*

NORA ROBERTS

"

CHAPTER 4

Your Flirting Language Speaks Volumes

USE YOUR WORDS TO MAKE AN UNFORGETTABLE FIRST IMPRESSION

For lots of us, the most challenging part of flirting is knowing what to say to a potential partner. It's way too easy to freeze—or bolt for the door—just when you want to introduce yourself to someone interesting. But this chapter will change that. I'm going to show you how what you say can create a positive, lasting connection with your flirting interest—in just about any situation. You'll learn how to work the room and meet new people at events, and I'll help you figure out what to say so you come across as naturally confident. Speaking of which, you'll learn how and why small talk is big, and how you can use it to spark interesting, meaningful conversations with the people you meet. And the best part is, you'll have a blast doing it!

WORK THE ROOM TO ATTRACT OTHERS INSTANTLY

I've never had any conventional hobbies like running, scuba diving, painting, or baking. Instead, my favorite pastime is working a room. I come alive at parties, conferences, networking events, charity functions—you name it! No matter how tired I am, put me in a room of strangers and I instantly perk up. I love meeting new people, finding out what makes them tick, what they like, where they live, what they do, who they know, what they enjoy, and so on. I love making strangers feel comfortable, making them laugh, and enjoying the spontaneity and adventure of connecting. I never know who I may meet or how they may enrich my life.

Sound like fun? It really is, and if you're convinced you'll never love socializing in big groups this way, I'm here to change your mind. First, though, what exactly is "working a room?" It's being able to mingle and socialize comfortably as you circulate among any gathering of people. And it's all about making connections. You'll create magical moments by approaching others as you establish a bond based on building rapport, trust, and kindness. If working a room makes you cringe and you get heart palpitations just thinking about it, never fear. All it takes is a little practice to become great at it.

RECALIBRATE YOUR MINDSET

Think of "working a room" as buying a lottery ticket. You've got to be in it to win it! It's all about the limitless possibilities you have when you connect with someone you don't know. So, put a positive spin on it. Any place in which you come into contact with new people is an ideal venue for meeting others for fun, friendship, romance, or a professional connection. You never know who you might meet when you work the room!

PREP BEFORE YOU ARRIVE

Believing in the benefits of working a room is essential! And that means you'll want to be in the right headspace for making new connections. Here are some pre-event rules that make working the room a breeze—whether you're at a party, a singles' event, a workshop, a conference, or a social function like a wedding or birthday party.

- Look your best. Being well groomed, smelling terrific, and wearing a smile are prerequisites.

- Select an outfit you feel confident in, and one that will get you noticed (a tasteful one, of course).

- Leave your baggage at home. This includes job worries, horror stories about your ex, and family drama.

- Focus on the anticipation of meeting potential dates. Get excited!

- Have your business cards easily accessible. (We'll talk more about this later.) If you don't have a business card, you can exchange Instagram or Twitter handles, email addresses, or you can simply say, "I'll text you so you have my phone number," or "Text me so I have your phone number."

- Brush up on the day's newsy items. Check out what's trending on Twitter, listen to the news or watch it on TV, or check your social media feeds to be up to date on the latest happenings.

- Give yourself a pep talk. Remind yourself that you are going out to meet new people and not just to talk to your best bud (if you're going with one). If you *do* go with a friend, make sure to communicate your strategy beforehand. (It may inspire him or her to adopt the same attitude!)

- Have an opening line handy. "What brings you here?" is a favorite of mine because it's open ended and often leads to establishing a shared interest. From there, you can talk about anything—the event, movies, schools you have attended, favorite restaurants, your occupation, or your funniest travel story.

SET THE MOOD

To do this, think of yourself as a pilot almost ready to land a plane. Doing the following will ensure a smooth, bump-free landing, and leave you feeling self-assured and ready to flirt.

- If possible, check your coat, backpack, briefcase, etc. Having your hands free gives you the freedom to mingle easily. Put your phone on vibrate, take off your headphones, put away your tablet, and you'll be ready to meet the other attendees.

- Arrive early so you can get comfortable with the venue, talk to other early-arrivers or the host, and prepare for the rest of the event. You are now someone who can welcome others just because you are already there!

- Give the room a once-over to scope out potential flirting partners and to become familiar with your surroundings. Pay attention to where you can sit, the location of food, drinks, the restrooms, and any other key spots. If you know something about the place, you'll have some tips to impart to your flirting interests. (Now you're the expert!)

- Remember, if you experience rejection, it will not destroy you. In fact, it's a gift: It frees you to mingle, circulate, and make new connections! (For a refresher on how to reframe rejection, see page 20.)

LET THE REAL FUN BEGIN

Okay, the event is in full swing, and you're ready to socialize! You look good and feel courageous. That's a great start!

When you move around the room, walk as if you have a destination but all the time in the world to get there.

Don't look like you're running to catch a bus or dragging yourself along after finishing a marathon. Instead, walk like you're the master of ceremonies or the guest of honor. Act as if you belong there, and are ecstatic to be there.

MAKE THE FIRST MOVE

Making the first move is tough, but failing to do so can set you back—in more than just your love life. If you don't make the first move, you might miss a great opportunity. Start by talking to someone who catches your eye, is standing alone, looks approachable, or happens to be sitting next to you—just about anyone.

Even though you may have butterflies in your stomach, just getting the words out will help mitigate the "anxiety minefield" that may be building inside you. Before you know it, the butterflies fade and your enjoyment of the moment increases. For instance, my friend Quinn is an outgoing person who still finds it difficult to make the first move when it comes to meeting new people. But at a recent networking event, she noticed a woman nearby who was looking in her direction. Quinn introduced herself, and the woman looked really relieved. She'd clearly been hoping that someone else would make the first move! Everyone's in the same boat at events like these; if you introduce yourself first, it's likely you'll be welcomed with open arms.

Everything gets easier after you deliver your opening line—and, flirting is a social skill that improves with practice and repetition. The more you do it, the greater your comfort level will be.

Finally, remember you are there to meet potential dates. If you spend half the evening plotting your first move, the event will be over before you know it and you still won't have spoken to a single soul. So, get moving!

PRACTICE BEING THE HOST

This is one of my favorite tips for working a room: Think of yourself as the event's host rather than a guest. Here's why: Playing host takes the focus off you and places it on your flirting interest. Your role as the host is to do anything and everything to make your "guest" feel welcome and accepted. For those who despise mingling, this is a great trick because it allows you to forget about your nerves and focus on your guests.

Next time you attend a gathering, try these party-hosting techniques:

- Introduce yourself. What's most important here, though, is that you simply *start talking*. Don't dwell too much on saying the "right" thing. Just get your mouth moving! Offer to get the person a drink, dessert, or to hold a seat for him.

- Once you start talking to someone, ask for a favor. "Could you grab me a napkin?" or, "Would you mind watching my seat for a moment?" It's a natural way to make her feel included, and it actually creates intimacy.

- Give the person extra space at a crowded event. ("Let me move over a bit to make you more comfortable.")

- Offer to help. ("I see you're waiting to get a drink. There's another less-crowded bar down the hall. Do you want to join me?")

If other people show interest in joining your conversation, invite them in. The more people you get to know, the greater your chances of finding someone you like.

MAKING A GRACEFUL (AND QUICK) EXIT

We've all been there: A conversation starts with promise, but, a few minutes in, it fizzles. You'd like to get away—either to meet other new people or because you simply can't stand it a second longer. In these situations, use any of the following get-away lines.

- "Sorry, I promised to meet up with a friend."

- "It's late. I've got to get going."

- "I'm going to walk around a bit. Have a good night."

- "I was actually just about to use the restroom. Take care."

- "Excuse me. I need to take this call/answer this text."

Keep it short and simple–don't feel you have to offer a lengthy explanation–and do so as soon as you feel the conversation going nowhere. We often "stick around" because we don't want to hurt the other person's feelings, but, in fact, the more you linger, the more you are leading him or her on.

YOUR FLIRTING CARD (A.K.A. BUSINESS CARD)

Let's say you've been talking to someone and the vibes and body language are looking good. All signs point to mutual interest. But, for some reason, one of you needs to leave. Now's the perfect time to say, "I'm having a great time with you and would love to get together. Here's my card."

It's much smoother than requesting a phone number. Someone who's into you will surely accept your card and offer one in return (or write down contact information for you). Someone who doesn't want to stay in touch will likely squirm, stutter, or do nothing. When this happens, smile, and say, "I see someone over there I need to talk with. It was nice meeting you." It's the perfect recipe for a graceful exit.

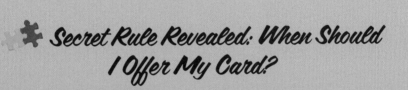

Secret Rule Revealed: When Should I Offer My Card?

Do this the moment you feel that spark that says, "I'd like to see you again." Making the request sooner than that looks creepy and desperate! And worse, it may suggest you want *anybody's* phone number, and that your flirting interest just happens to be the one for now. Don't rush it: Trust your gut and wait for the right moment.

What If I Don't Have a Business Card?

Business cards are great for making professional and social connections because of their practicality; they offer a simple way to exchange information.

If you don't have a card, or feel reluctant handing one out because it contains all your work information, get *flirting cards* made instead. These should include your name and contact info, like your phone number, email address, and Twitter or Instagram handle. You can personalize your flirting card by selecting a clear, eye-catching font, an unusual color, or a unique logo or design.

Because business cards typically say what you do, a card without that information will spark conversation about your work life. If you feel silly having a card with only your name and contact information, consider adding a line that hints at your profession or passion—for example, "consultant," "chef," "avid . . .," "coach," or "chocoholic." This can help spark an interesting conversation—even if you're not working. Alternatively, you can suggest connecting right then and there on Twitter, Instagram, or LinkedIn, or do it the old-fashioned way and exchange phone numbers (or "coordinates," as a friend of mine phrases it!).

Finally, no matter what type of card you have, have it handy so you're not digging around in your pocket or handbag in search of one!

SHOULD I FLY SOLO OR WITH A WINGPERSON?

Being half a team when you work a room can make flirting seem easier. That way, the two of you can walk over to your flirting interests and strike up a conversation. It may even seem more natural or fun that way. Conversely, an upbeat, entertaining conversation between you and your pal could invite others to join in (assuming you keep yourselves open to the crowd).

So, here's my advice: If flying duo gives you wings to work the room, go for it! But if flying duo makes you stick to your friend like glue, solo sailing is the answer for you.

A third option is to arrive at the event with your wingperson, hang out together for a bit to bolster your confidence, and then work the room *solo*. If you decide on this option, here's the plan:

- Spend ten minutes talking to each other.

- Make a plan to head your separate flirting ways, but, before you part, decide on a check-in time. Your time frame will depend largely on the length of the event; at a two-hour singles' event, for example, you may meet up after thirty minutes. At a bar or party, it may be after just fifteen minutes.

- At your check-in, decide what time you will leave the event.

- Enjoy working the room! By the night's end, you'll surely have some great stories to share with your friend. Maybe you'll have met someone you'd like to see again— or maybe your friend will have met the perfect person for you—or vice versa!

MASTERING THE ART OF SMALL TALK: TURN AWKWARD MOMENTS INTO GENUINE CONNECTIONS

How much does a polar bear weigh? Enough to break the ice!

Are you smiling or rolling your eyes right now? You're probably doing both, because I captured your attention, didn't I? Great! That's exactly what I wanted to do.

One secret of being a superb flirt is ensuring that your words and your actions complement each other. And I'm going to show you how to do just that. You will learn how to combine the techniques from chapter 2—eye contact, distance, smile, touch, mirroring, the flirtatious handshake, and so on—with verbal styles to wow even the most standoffish and reserved person.

SMALL TALK IS HUGE: NEVER BE AT A LOSS FOR WORDS

Your attitude about small talk is like having the flu: It's highly contagious! The more you believe that every conversation is a potential gift and an opportunity for the unexpected, the better you will be at it. Think of small talk as the introduction to a book, the appetizer at a great meal, or the beginning of your next love affair. After all, every relationship starts with a single conversation. And small talk is anything but small: It always focuses on making the person you are talking to feel cared for, valued, and listened to, which means it has a massive effect. As the other person's comfort level rises, he or she will open up to you and small talk will become meaningful conversation.

THE BEST OPENING LINES TO BREAK THE ICE

Great opening lines fit like a glove; they're like your favorite pair of sweats, most comfortable pair of shoes, or your most beat-up jeans: You feel totally at ease in them! When you have a great opening line that works, use and reuse it to your heart's content (as long as you use it on different people, that is).

Let's start with the basics. First of all, an opening line is a statement or question that captures the attention of your flirting interest. It can be funny, intriguing, or complimentary. Opening lines create a fabulous first impression and help establish a warm connection.

SHED YOUR OPENING LINE BUTTERFLIES

Have you ever spent ten minutes obsessing over crafting the "ultimate" opening line—only to look around and see that your flirting interest is nowhere to be found? If you find yourself in this dilemma, remember that any opening line, even a mediocre one, is worth trying. When worrying starts to overcome your thoughts, remind yourself that saying anything is better than nothing.

We have all experienced a *flirting freeze moment* when, instead of making the first move, we clam up and go mute. This is especially common when we are super

attracted to our flirting interest—as the stakes increase, our anxiety grows as well (go figure!). Get out of the deep freeze by facing your fear. Just start talking! I promise the jitters will fade as your conversation takes off.

Lastly, everyone worries about not getting the exact response they want from their flirting interest. That's normal. Remember that rejection is actually a gift: You didn't waste any more time talking to someone who's not interested, and now you're free to move on. That's a win!

ENTICE YOUR FLIRTING INTEREST WITH THESE ANTI-PICK-UP LINES

Did you know, the best pick-up lines are "anti-pick-up lines?" Let me explain. No one wants to be on the receiving end of a line that feels like it's been used and overused. It'll be ignored, and that's not what you want. The options listed here will help you craft your own out-of-the-ordinary opening line.

1 Keep It Simple: Just Say, "Hi"

By far, the best opening line is a confident, animated "hi" or "hello." Why is it so effective? Because we're all so used to staring at our phones that saying "hi" is a daring move in today's techie world. And you don't have to worry about coming up with a clever one-liner: All you need is the guts to say a single word. Pair "hi" with warm eye contact, a big smile, and a quick introduction. Who could resist?

2 Pay a Compliment

Compliments make great opening lines because everyone loves to be noticed and to be told something affirming. It makes people feel special and secure.

From my collection of opening-line strategies, using compliments is my all-time favorite. It is the most natural way to start a conversation, and it always generates unanticipated outcomes. And it sets a positive, upbeat tone. When I receive a compliment from a stranger, I beam from ear to ear. It's instant happiness.

What makes a phenomenal compliment? First, it's honest, genuine, and sincere. Your flirting interest will see right through one that's not, will feel

🧩 Secret Rule Revealed: Ask Creative, Insightful Questions

The real secret: You don't need a pickup line! Questions build connections and facilitate conversation. I've outlined here my tried-and-true examples. Be adventurous, mix and match, and devise some of your own to reflect your personality.

uncomfortable, and your encounter will come to a screeching halt.

Second, the best compliments have the element of surprise coupled with specificity. This conveys that you have really paid attention to him, and want to let him know it! Hearing the same compliment time and again is nice—but it's nothing special. Then you receive an unexpected compliment, and—wow—it feels amazing. Here are some examples of first-rate compliments:

- To a woman in a supermarket: "I can tell you're [the perfect party host/the best baker/the most amazing Italian cook] by all the good stuff in your cart! What's your specialty?"

- To a man standing in line next to you: "I am impressed by the fact that you seem completely unfazed that this line is taking forever."

- To a woman standing in a bar: "You were so kind to that frenzied bartender."

- To a man talking to his friend: "I couldn't help overhearing your conversation; you sound like such a cooking expert—and I could seriously use some tips."

3 Use Your Surroundings as a Conversation Starter

Imagine you're at a party, waiting in line, at the airport, in a store, taking a class, or doing just about anything. You see someone who catches your eye. You really want to meet that person. But you get nervous and still don't know what to say. All your great opening lines have deserted you, and you need to come up with something—fast!

Look around you. Your surroundings will supply many conversation topics. Think about what you see, hear, notice, even smell.

Check out anything and everything, from the wallpaper to the coffee's aroma to the way people are dressed to the anticipation you feel about the show that's about to start. Then comment on it. Talk about the people, the food, the décor, the host, the wait, the price of gas, the item in the store you can't find, the instructor–anything!

Think of your surroundings as your flirting first-aid rescue. Use them to stay in the moment and connect with your flirting interest. After all, you already have something in common– you are waiting in line together, taking the same class, or are guests at the same party. Use that to your advantage with a witty or upbeat comment.

4 Ask Phenomenal Questions

What can you do if you feel shy or unsure of yourself but don't want to miss out on a flirting op? Ask a flirtatious question! They jumpstart the conversation and determine whether the initial attraction will live on. (Getting an answer to your question is a bonus!)

5 Say "Goodbye" Instead of "Hello"

Huh? Didn't I just tell you how to introduce yourself to your flirting interest? I know this sounds like a contradiction, but it can work if:

- You've spent the whole evening building up your courage to say "hi" but never did.
- Your flirting interest arrives as you leave.
- You didn't get a chance to approach your flirting interest, and now the event is over or the venue is closing.

In these situations. Say, "Hi. I was on my way out, but I didn't want to leave without introducing myself. I'm [your name]." Then you might want to delay your departure if your goodbye turns out to be a success!

At places you frequent, such as the gym, coffee shop, school, or dog park, you could just say, "Bye! Have a good day/weekend," and when you see the person again, say, "Good to see you," followed by a compliment or question.

It might seem counterintuitive at first, but saying goodbye can be as good a way to make an introduction as saying hello!

WHEN A CURVE BALL COMES YOUR WAY

Just as you're finding the right words to approach your flirting interest, the waiter drops food on your lap, everything falls out of your purse, or you realize you left home without your wallet as you try to pay for your breakfast. Great! The universe has just handed you a perfect opening line. Use it to impress your flirting interest. Turning lemons into lemonade can be so sweet!

Secret Rule Revealed: Transform Your Question from Dull to Dynamic

Have you ever asked someone a question to break the ice, and knew that it was a dead-end question as soon as you asked it? Don't worry: You can recover. Even if you asked a boring question, turn it around by reacting quickly. Respond to your flirting interest's answer in a fun and playful way. Here are few examples:

YOUR QUESTION: "How are you?"

HIS ANSWER: "Good."

YOUR RESPONSE: "That's great, because I'm a whole lot better now that we've met. I'm [your name]. It's so nice to meet you."

YOUR QUESTION: "Do you know what the best appetizers in this restaurant are?"

HER ANSWER: "No, sorry, I don't."

YOUR RESPONSE: "I'd love to know what your favorite appetizers are and I promise to tell you mine!"

Cheat Sheet: Questions That Will Get You Noticed

TYPE OF QUESTION	SAMPLE SITUATIONS AND QUESTIONS
STARTER QUESTIONS: A starter question that takes off will lead to an awesome conversation.	• **At a social gathering:** "Hi, I'm Debbie's cousin. Who do you know here?" or "Who did you come with?" • **At a seminar:** "What do you think of the PowerPoint so far?" • **In the produce section of a grocery store:** "Do you know how to pick a sweet pineapple?" • **In the bookstore:** "Any suggestions on a great book for my colleague?" • **In a hotel lobby:** "You have a great accent. Where are you from?" • **In a bar:** "That looks delicious. May I ask what you're drinking?" • **In line at the grocery store:** "Would you mind watching my spot while I grab something from the next aisle?"
ENGAGING QUESTIONS: As the name suggests, these questions dig deeper. We all love to talk about ourselves, so fire away with questions that will get your flirting interest talking!	• **"What's your favorite ...** [ice cream/food/ TV movie/ reality show]?" • **"What do you think of ...** [particular sports team/ news topic/car type]?" • **"What would you do if you ...** [were late for a date and didn't have your cell phone/found $100/got a great job in another country?]" • **"What are you most passionate about ...** [hobbies/ work/charity]?"

FUN QUESTIONS: Amusing, humorous, or comical questions get the other person laughing and ease nerves simultaneously.	• "Are you superstitious about anything?" • "Do you floss before or after you brush?" • "How are your socks arranged in your drawer?"
UNUSUAL QUESTIONS: Out-of-the-ordinary, inquisitive questions lend themselves to interesting dialog and thought-provoking conversation.	• "What is the funniest or most interesting item in your pocket or purse?" • "How did you get your name?" • "What makes you laugh?" • "What is something I would never guess about you?"
RELATIONSHIP-STATUS QUESTIONS: These questions find out whether your flirting interest is married or taken.	• "Did your significant other get you that eye-catching watch?" • "What kind of work does your partner do?" • "Does your girlfriend/boyfriend like [whatever you are doing ... watching sports/eating sushi/playing tennis] as much as you do?" • "Did your wife pick out that gorgeous sweater?" • "Should I guess how long you've been married?"
HELP QUESTIONS: These questions ask for help and show you value his or her knowledge or skill. Once you get the help you need, follow it up with a thank you, compliment, or an offer to return the favor!	• **At a bar:** "Could you help me get the bartender's attention?" • **At a store:** "Any suggestions for a gift for a five-year-old/great aunt/neighbor/colleague?" • **At a class (or after):** "I didn't catch what the instructor said. Would you mind explaining it to me?" • **At a train station:** "Can you help me figure out the schedule app/What's the best way to get to ... ?"

FLIRTING FAUX PAS: INNOCENT WORDS CAN BECOME A FLIRTING NIGHTMARE

Have you ever regretted saying something the second it came out of your mouth? Something you knew instantly ruined the moment? We all have, and, when this happens, it's best to have a strategy for a quick recovery (or better yet, prevent it from happening at all).

Following are a few opening-line disasters to avoid at all costs, plus a few strategies to use in case of a slip up. Remember, anything is fixable.

Stay away from opening lines with a negative spin. I can assure you that your flirting interest will become defensive or irritated. No matter how innocent your intentions, the outcome will not be good. Here are some examples of what not to say:

- "What's someone like you doing in a place like this?" or "You don't look like you belong in a place like this." (A confusing conversation killer.)

- "Didn't you have anything better to do tonight than come here?" (Insulting and a put-down.)

- "Still haven't met anyone? I've seen you at this singles' event lots of times." (A personal dig—and hurtful!)

- "You're so dressed up for this event." (Confusing and uncomfortable.)

If you find yourself accidentally saying something you wish you hadn't, here's how you can quickly turn the calamity into a valuable flirting opportunity.

First, apologize. Say you did not mean to offend, and rephrase your question into a compliment. For example, after saying, "You're so dressed up," make amends by saying, "I'm sorry, what I really meant to say was that your dress is absolutely amazing." Or after saying, "Still haven't met anyone?" quickly recover with, "Sorry, do over! What I meant was I'm glad you're here tonight because I wanted to introduce myself to you a few weeks ago but didn't get the opportunity. Great to see you!"

BTW, if you are the receiver of any of these kinds of opening lines, help save the day by putting a positive spin on your response!

LISTENING MAKES YOU THE BEST CONVERSATIONALIST

Once you have his or her attention, you start talking. Now, listening becomes the golden rule.

It's no biological accident that we have two ears and one mouth. It means you should listen twice as much as you talk. This may seem impossible, but it is essential.

To understand the importance of listening, think about how you feel when someone listens intently to you. With eyes and ears tuned to you—and only you—you feel like a superstar, like the center of the universe. That's a feeling worth reciprocating, right?

Listening is one of the most valuable parts of the flirting communication process because it creates an interpersonal bond. When you feel that someone has heard you and truly understands your words and your feelings, you form a connection—and you never want the conversation to end!

THE ESSENTIALS OF LISTENING

Listening is not a passive process. It's as active and alive as talking. It can be exciting and scary when someone you've had your eye on approaches you. Take a few deep breaths and erase your mind's competing emotions. In this case, a one-track mind *is* your goal. It's even okay to share your feelings. (He or she might be feeling the same way.) Our minds wander (whether we like it or not). As soon as this happens, quickly say, "Sorry, I just missed what you said." This is a simple technique to convey that you are seriously interested in what he is saying. And, please don't pretend to understand something if you are clueless about what just came out of his mouth. Asking for a repeat or explanation is a great way to give your flirting interest a chance to shine!

BE A DYNAMIC, ACTIVE LISTENER IN THREE STEPS

1 Give Your Undivided Attention

Remember, it is much better to be *interested* than *interesting*, so always stay in the "hear" and now! Give your flirting partner your undivided attention by maintaining eye contact and proper distance, and, above all else, listening closely to what is being said. Finally, no matter how great the temptation to plan your response, don't do it. It's so much easier to be spontaneous and playful when you respond to what was just said.

Secret Rule Revealed: Demonstrate Admiration

Expressing admiration is a real turn-on. You can't admire someone if you don't listen!

Here are my top tips for giving your undivided attention:

- Laugh at funny comments.
- Try your best not to interrupt.
- Move in closer to show you don't want to miss a word.
- Maintain eye contact to demonstrate you are following the conversation.
- Block out distractions around you.
- Avoid quick glances at your watch or phone.

2 Offer Instantaneous Feedback

This is really important. Your flirting interest cannot read your mind, but can read your signals. This means you should provide immediate feedback. Don't make the other person speculate; it ruins the flirting flow.

Keep your listening feedback simple, using one or more words from this list: "Yes," "Yeah," "Uh-huh," "I see," "Oh," "Really," and "Wow!" These communicate that you are listening, and encourage your flirting interest to continue. Just remember that timing with these words is important. Saying "yes" or "uh-huh" every once in a while works well; saying it every two seconds can irritate and grate on someone's nerves. Practice moderation.

You can also respond with a few words related to what's being said or request more information. For example, "I totally agree," "How interesting," "I can't believe that happened," "I'm not sure I'm following what you are saying. Could you explain that?" or "Please tell me more."

3 Paraphrase What Your Flirting Interest Said

During a lull or natural pause in the conversation, repeat what your flirting interest said to keep the conversation engaging and remind your crush that you're really interested. Restate what she said *in your own words*. Make sure you also paraphrase the feelings as well, if appropriate. It will warm her heart.

For example, if your flirting interest says, "My GPS took me to the ferry because it was the closest route instead of taking me to the freeway. I can't believe I actually took my car on the ferry." You say, "How funny! Who would have imagined that a car could swim? What a great story!" When you paraphrase or summarize what your flirting interest says in this way, you pay the greatest compliment—showing genuine interest and concern.

USE FLIRTING PROPS TO GET NOTICED AND START CONVERSATIONS

A prop is an accessory that makes a personal statement. It gets others' attention and invites flirting prospects to talk to you. That's why you should never leave home without one.

Props work so well because they give others the chance to talk to you about something *tangible*, rather than simply pulling a topic out of thin air. That's right: Props make it easier for *other people* to make the first move *on you*. All you have to do is respond and flirt back with interest and energy. I told you it was easy!

THE TOP NINE FLIRTING PROPS

1 Jewelry with Pizazz

Unique, unusual, or even classic jewelry will encourage others to comment. In a nutshell, if it makes you stand out, it is the perfect prop. Likewise, if you have a favorite jewelry piece or one you have received compliments on in the past, incorporate it into your prop pile.

Your jewelry "prop" could be old, new, trendy, timeless, crafty, expensive, or a super bargain. It could be a bracelet made out of paper clips from your six-year-old daughter; an antique necklace or a neon pink one; a watch passed down from your great-grandfather; or a sparkling bracelet you designed yourself. Basically, any jewelry that complements or enhances your outfit can act as a conversation piece.

In my opinion, a watch is the greatest jewelry prop of all—for men and women alike. A watch is the most frequently noticed piece of jewelry because asking the time is a natural way to start a conversation.

Here are a few more examples of jewelry that will stimulate curiosity and small talk. Adapt any of these suggestions to fit your personal jewelry style. Just remember—dare to be different. It will get you noticed.

- A pin that showcases your profession or passion (i.e., a dog if you are a groomer; a military insignia if you've served)

- A necklace with a charm that showcases something you love (e.g., a pair of flip-flops to symbolize that you love summer or the beach)

- A bracelet made out of an antique spoon

- A diving watch, a Disney watch, or a smartwatch

- A trendy piece of jewelry

2 Personalized Clothing

Have you ever started a conversation with someone wearing a T-shirt or hat with the name of a place you've visited or a school you attended? That's because the clothing instantaneously gives you common ground—no opening line needed.

Wearing clothing that signifies something about you, with your alma mater or your town name, gives your flirting prospect a green light to start talking to you, and gives others a little insight into you

Man Props: Ties, Suspenders, Belts, Jewelry, and Socks

When it comes to flirting props, attention-grabbing ties or bow ties are a man's best friend. Look for well-made silk ties that go well with a suit. Splurge on a few and don't be afraid to wear colorful or unusual bow ties for a change of pace—you want them to get noticed. The same goes for suspenders (if that's more your style)—the funkier, the better! Belts with unusual buckles or super-soft leather can spark a connection, while an out-of-the ordinary earring, an unusual ring, or a cool watch are all perfect man props, as well. Even unconventional socks are a conversation starter. Just don't wear all your props at the same time!

and your interests. If your flirting wardrobe lacks these personalized items, add at least one or two pieces. The best flirting clothing includes items with any of the following:

- A place or sightseeing attraction you have visited (e.g., Rome's Coliseum or the Grand Canyon)

- An organization to which you belong (e.g., Wounded Warriors or a union)

- An activity club in which you participate (e.g., a triathlon or photography club)

- A cause meaningful to you (e.g., saving the environment or fighting breast cancer)

- A hobby or passion (e.g., movie buff, dancing, or classic cars)

- A school you attend(ed)

People who share the passions or affiliations your clothing displays will naturally feel more comfortable around you because you already have a bond. And don't forget to wear these items when traveling or on vacation—it's even more fun to get noticed when you are away from home.

3 Your Scent

According to a study in the journal *PLOS One*, women's faces were perceived as being more attractive if a pleasant smell was present. Studies from the Smell & Taste Treatment and Research Foundation show that women who dabbed a bit of pink grapefruit juice behind their earlobes were perceived as five years younger than their actual age! Don't you automatically tend to see people as more attractive if they smell delicious? (I do!) Some of the scents men are drawn to are citrus, vanilla, and coconut.

Smelling good makes us feel appealing and our natural scent is often our best scent. You don't want your scent to linger in the elevator hours after you've been there or be the reason your flirting interest has an asthma attack! A great way to smell terrific and not overdo it is to either spray your perfume about twelve inches (30 cm) in front of you and walk into it, or give yourself a spray or two on your wrists and neck, or spritz your hair. It'll inspire your flirting interest to tell you how much he likes your scent!

> **A perfume is something which is invisible and yet an unforgettable accessory.**
>
> **COCO CHANEL**

Your scent is your signature because it's based on personal preference. The perfect scent is the one that makes you feel alluring, happy, and a little sexy! Scents have an intense connection with memory; therefore, your flirting partner will think of you when she smells your fragrance, even if she smells it on someone else. What a great way to leave a lasting impression!

4 Manicured Nails

People notice your hands all the time—that's why having well-manicured nails will take you far. It's a sign that you value your appearance and take pride in yourself.

A manicure doesn't always equal painted nails. For guys, this means keeping your nails clean and trimmed. For ladies, the same thing goes, but you may also consider a French manicure, sheer polish, seasonal color, nail jewelry, or a subtle design. A professional manicure may be one of your best flirting investments.

5 Shopping Bags, Totes, and Umbrellas

You probably need to carry a few of these items anyway, so why not make them unique? Try a shopping bag from a specialty shop, a tote from a conference you attended, or a colorful umbrella.

He is much more likely to strike up a conversation if your tote conveys the name of something he relates to or can identify with. (This works all the time for my friend Jess: People always comment on her tote bag from Alaska that features a photo of Pike Place Fish Market and her shopping bag from a very high-end restaurant in New York City.)

6 Fresh Flowers

Whenever I see someone buying flowers—especially at a supermarket, outdoor market, or a location other than a florist—I'm delighted, because it's such a natural conversation starter. You can comment on the flowers, or on how lucky the recipient will be. You could playfully say, "Aw, how nice of you to get me flowers!" or "Oh, you shouldn't have!" My friend Megan told me that every time she brings someone flowers and finds herself walking around with them, she gets a ton of comments from both men and women—both on the street and in bars and restaurants. They ask her if it's her birthday or if she's going to visit someone in the hospital. Try it yourself: Buy yourself some flowers and carry them around with you for a few hours. You might be surprised at what happens!

7 Reading Material

Ever been reading on a plane or train and had someone comment on your literary selection? It happens all the time, right? That's why reading material makes the perfect prop—it shows others two of your interests: reading and the subject about which you're reading. Plus, it invites recommendations.

Choose a book, magazine, or newspaper that interests you. It could be a textbook, this book, a rare magazine, a journal to which you subscribe, poetry by your favorite poet, or a current best seller—the more out of the ordinary, or trendy, the better. You never know; the next time you carry your favorite book may be the most memorable experience of your life.

8 Friendly Pups

If you have a pet—or don't mind walking your friend's—this one is a winner. Dogs are like best friends: They are so easy to talk to—and make great listeners!

A pooch is a great flirting accessory because people who stop to admire or pet your dog already show you that you have something in common—your love for canines. As she talks to Fido, chime in with questions about whether she owns a pet or her favorite breed.

If you don't have one, offer your dog-walking services to your friends. You'll not only be helpful, but you may even get a date out of it.

9 Kids

Children under the age of five are natural flirts—everyone wants to get a smile out of them! With kids around, there is so much to talk about, especially if the other person has a child, as well. After chatting about your kids, it's easy to move the conversation to you, your relation-ship status, your interests, and so on.

If you don't have small children and you are a capable, responsible babysitter, consider taking a niece or nephew, grandchild, godchild, or friend's child out for an afternoon at the mall, park, or playground. You'll have fun no matter what.

PROPS GO BOTH WAYS

Props can work both ways. Instead of waiting for others to comment about your props, why not comment on theirs? It's an easy, fun way to kickstart a conversation. And who doesn't love talking about him or herself?

EASY PROP-RELATED QUESTIONS YOU CAN ASK

Think of another person's prop as your cue card—it tells you what to say. Although you don't have a script, consider props as clues to solving a puzzle. The more questions you ask, the more information you get, and the better the flirting becomes. And, as you learn more about the other person, you will find more topics in common and the conversation gets better and better.

Here are some examples of great ways to use props as conversation starters:

- "Your necklace is stunning. Where did you get it?"

- "Did you go to the University of Toronto? I have the same T-shirt."

- "Are you wearing [name of cologne]? You smell so nice."

- "I just love the design on your nails. Where do you get them done?"

- "Where did you find that laptop case? It looks great, and so functional, too."

- "How are you finding that book so far? I had a hard time getting into it at first but ended up loving it."

- "Your dog is beautiful! Where do you get her groomed?"

Now that you're unlikely to be at a loss for words, you'll want to know where to use your newfound skills! In the next chapter, I'll share the most fun and unusual places to flirt and date. Read on!

> Courage doesn't mean you don't get afraid. Courage means you *don't let fear stop you.*

BETHANY HAMILTON

CHAPTER 5

Where to Flirt

THE IDEAL FLIRTING VENUES AND THE BEST DATE IDEAS

I'm about to share with you the most valuable rule of flirting, which I've learned through years of practice. Let me get straight to the point: The best place to flirt is *wherever you are right now*! You can flirt day or night, close to home or across the globe, when you least expect it, when you're doing your everyday "stuff," like chores or errands, or at a one-time event. *No* place is off limits—even when you're visiting someone at the hospital or waiting in line for a restroom. Seriously! I don't ever want you to pass up an opportunity to make a social, business, or love connection.

This chapter takes you through my thirty favorite flirting venues, all based on the amazing stories I've been told by thousands of flirting workshop participants, by the men and women I have interviewed while doing research for this book, and on my very own flirting missions.

Not a day goes by in which I haven't flirted several times in multiple locations. I can't help myself: It fills my day with new adventures and connections. And there's no reason you can't do the same! You'll add fun and excitement to your life and you'll make someone else's day a whole lot sweeter. I call that a win-win.

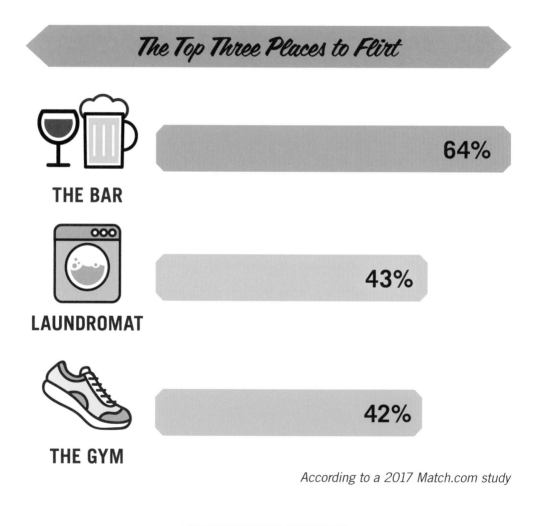

The Top Three Places to Flirt

THE BAR — 64%

LAUNDROMAT — 43%

THE GYM — 42%

According to a 2017 Match.com study

THIRTY OF THE BEST PLACES TO FLIRT

Now it's time to put all your flirting skills into action. The following alphabetical list is varied because I want you to have a wide range of options when it comes to flirting. For starters, zero in on the places that match your personality and lifestyle— but don't stop. (You'll miss out on so many great flirting moments if you do!)

Your goal is to flirt at as many different venues as possible, even if they are outside your comfort zone. For example, if flirting in line, at the gym, or in a doctor's waiting room seems off limits for you, I specifically want you to flirt at those locations. You already know that if you keep doing the same things you'll get the same results, so be brave and adventurous and push the envelope a bit! Select locations from this list that you find challenging, scary, or are simply brand new to you. Often, trying something new has the most positive outcome. And it would be great if you tried all thirty! Tell me your favorite places to flirt. Send me pics of where you're flirting on Instagram @lovebugFran.

1. AIRPORTS AND AIRPLANES

Turn an aggravating airport delay or a four-hour flight into a thrilling flirting adventure. Your shared destination already gives you something in common. You can become instant friends during your wait to board or during your flight together.

2. BARS, PUBS, AND CLUBS

Whether it's your neighborhood pub, an after-work happy hour, 40+ Thursdays, or Margarita Mondays, you can always find a reason to go, and you don't even have to drink: You can just nurse a club soda and lime all night! Find a spot at the bar, order a drink, and talk to the people around you. Work the bar by walking around as if you are going somewhere, and stop and talk when you exchange a smile or eye contact.

Meetup Groups

Meetup.com is an online social-networking site that enables you to find a group in your area that interests you. All you have to do is enter your city and you will find groups related to careers, hobbies, health, politics, entertainment, sports, being single, and lots more. In 2017, there were 32 million users in approximately 182 countries, so you're likely to find a group that's right for you wherever you are. Try it—and you can even start your own meetup. (It's free for users, but organizers pay a fee.)

Similarly, MEETin.org is a website created to bring people together for casual, free, fun, social events. If the group meets for dinner or drinks, each member pays their own expenses. It is run by volunteers in ninety cities worldwide and has more than 90,000 members.

3. BEACH

Where there's water, there's flirting. Head for the beach, lake, or town pool–either solo or with a friend. Wear sunscreen with a delicious scent, and don't forget your props (magazines or a book, water toys, or even a beach towel from your company or school). Spend some time at the concession stand, too–it's always a great place to meet someone.

4. BOOKSTORE

Bookstores provide the perfect milieu: There are endless props to discuss; lots of people browse by themselves; there's often a café to grab a cup of coffee; there are places to sit, and they often host events such as book signings. It has the vibe of a casual meeting place, so it's one of the best locations to practice your flirting skills. I often take clients to bookstores so they can try out their skills or watch me in action.

The next time you're at a bookstore, walk around the entire store and scope it out. When you spot a flirting prospect, start looking at similar books and start a conversation about them. Ask for help selecting a book or offer your opinion about a book in his hand. If seats are scarce in the café, ask if she would mind sharing the table.

5. CLASS

It could be freshman orientation, your graduate chemistry course, a professional development workshop, water aerobics, Thai cooking, or CPR. Talk with a flirting interest before, during (quietly, of course), or after class. If you get a thumbs-up, suggest going for a drink, coffee, or a bite to eat to discuss what you just learned.

6. COMMUTER TRAINS AND BUSES

Feeling a bit shy about talking to a person waiting for the same train or the person that always sits in the seat in front of you? Try this! Today, smile as you're waiting; tomorrow, say hi; the next day, start a conversation.

Flirt Right Now

Don't wait for the "perfect time" or a special occasion to flirt. Flirts on the prowl make flirting a way of life. No matter where you are or what you're doing, flirting will bring you joy (and possibly love!) and will certainly enrich your life with amazing people you meet.

7. DOG PARK

Dog lovers seek out dog parks where their canine companions can have fun. This puts their owners in a similar frame of mind. Grab your dog (or a friend's dog) and go for some exercise–just don't forget to say hi to the pups and their owners, as well. Make nice to the pooch– and the pooch's human, too!

8. ELECTRONICS AND HARDWARE STORES

Men flock to these stores. If you need the latest electronic gadget or a long-lasting lightbulb, skip Amazon and go where they go. (You might even click with an engaging salesperson.)

9. FAST-FOOD PLACES, RESTAURANTS, COFFEE SHOPS

Fast-food places and coffee shops attract people dining alone. If you sit down next to a solo diner and feel like flirting, go for it! At a busy restaurant with a long wait time, forget about your hunger pains and ask what he likes best on the menu, strike up a conversation about the wait, or just say, "Hi, I'm [your name]," and start chatting. Remember no strings attached. (PS: if you go to a restaurant alone and there's a communal dining table, take advantage of it! Sit down as if the other diners are your friends, not strangers.)

10. FLEA MARKET, STREET FAIR, FARMERS' MARKET, OR GARAGE SALE

As you stroll and browse, don't forget to check out your flirting prospects along the way. Without a doubt, this is nirvana when it comes to flirting. Starting a conversation with a customer who looks interesting or a vendor who looks like your type will feel incredibly natural because there is so much around you to talk about. You can banter as you bargain for the best price, or teasingly say, "I will tell everyone at the street fair that you have the best collection of . . . if you . . .!" Ask about the stories behind the goods or how they got into it; tell them how it reminds you of your childhood or how creative it is. If there are food vendors, lucky you: Comment on the delicious smells, or say aloud, "Wow, everything looks scrumptious!" You never know: Someone interesting might respond!

Also, never miss an opportunity to start chatting with someone looking at the same things you are. Ask for an opinion, share what you know about the items she's admiring, and offer suggestions about other vendors.

11. FUNERALS

Although a funeral can be a very somber event, it's a place where everyone knows the deceased, which lends itself to talking to people you don't know. Especially if the funeral is a celebration of someone's life and the departed was a fun-loving, full-of-life individual—flirting could be a tribute to that person. That said, paying your respects to the bereaved is certainly first and foremost.

12. GYM OR PARK

The gym, walking course, or park is an ideal location for flexing your flirting muscles. Even if you see someone who catches your eye but neither of you makes a move this time, chances are you will see him again.

When you do, say something like, "Hi, I saw you (yesterday, last week, etc.), and wanted to say hi, but didn't. I'm [your name]," or, "I saw you a few days ago and wanted to ask where you got your sunblock shirt; it is exactly what I am looking for." If that seems too direct, ask for help with a particular machine, talk about your workout routine, or compliment the other person on her fitness ability or dedication.

13. HOTEL BARS, RESTAURANTS, OR LOBBIES

Hotels attract visitors from near and far for business and pleasure. Since business guests often travel alone, they are generally more open to meeting someone. It's also a great opportunity to make a work or social connection. Hotel guests on vacation enjoy meeting new people. Ask for restaurant recommendations, ask people where they are from, find out what sights they have seen, what kind of work they do, where else they have traveled. Showing genuine interest and sharing information about yourself is a perfect flirting duo.

14. JURY DUTY

Jury duty can be deadly or divine—it's your choice. Take advantage of the captive audience. Find a jury buddy and enjoy getting to know each other, and even grab lunch together. You never know where it may lead, and it's sure to make a boring day (or few days) much more exciting.

15. LAUNDROMAT

First, do a subtle check to see what's in his laundry basket. Depending on what you see, you will know how to proceed. If you determine the laundry contains only his clothing, feel free to offer your folding assistance, stain-removal tips, fabric softener, or some flirtatious conversation.

16. MALL

Ask directions for a store that you "can't find" (I won't tell). Ladies, go to the men's department and seek advice on "athletic wear for your nephew." Men, go to the ladies' department and ask for help selecting a "gift for your cousin's graduation." Go to a store that you love, even if you don't need anything. It's a great place to meet someone with similar tastes. Go to the food court and start chatting about each other's shopping expeditions.

17. MUSEUMS, ART GALLERIES, AND EXHIBITS

Museums and other cultural venues offer so much—art, history, and many potential flirting interests. Pay as much attention to the priceless paintings as you do the attendees! Then start talking. Ask a flirting interest about the exhibit or remark on the lifelike qualities of the manne-quins. While you're complimenting the works of art, compliment your flirting prospect as well.

18. NETWORKING OR BUSINESS EVENTS, TRADE SHOWS, AND CONVENTIONS

These are perfect places to hand out your business cards and make both professional and personal connections. When the opportunity arises (and only if appropriate), subtly let your business contacts know you are single, available, and would welcome an introduction from them. That could be the perfect time for your contact to say, "Actually, I'm available, too!"

19. OUTDOORS: PARKS, FESTIVALS, AND CONCERTS

These venues are full of people having a good time and getting some fresh air—and you can't ask for a more positive ambiance than that! If you see someone who looks friendly and approachable, don't be afraid to start a conversation, because you already have something in common—the art, the music, or the scenery. You never know where it could lead!

20. PARTIES

Parties are perfect for flirting: There's food, wine, something to celebrate, new people to meet (and those whom you already know), the mood is social, and the atmosphere is fun! Don't wait for others to come to you. Pretend you're a second host, be outgoing, and make others feel welcome. Your good vibes will draw others to you.

21. PLACES OF WORSHIP

Flirting where you feel comfortable makes flirting fun! Many sanctuaries have services or events for singles.

22. SCHOOL REUNIONS AND ALUMNI EVENTS

Even if you feel hesitant to attend, go! You never know who will be there, or who you will reconnect with. Plus, it's always great to find out what happened to your secret crush or old flame, isn't it?

23. SINGLES' EVENTS

Even before you get to the event, remind yourself not to wait for someone to approach you. Instead, take charge of your social life and start a conversation. You have made the effort to attend the event, now cash in on the love that could be waiting for you!

24. SPEED DATING

Because you only have a few minutes to get to know your "date," focus on making her feel special in your presence. Listen, ask questions, and compliment her. Before the bell rings to move on to the next date, make it clear you are interested (only if you are!). You can say, "I'm so glad I met you," or "I almost stayed home tonight, am I glad I didn't!"

25. SPORTS-RELATED ACTIVITIES

Whether you are watching an event, participating in one, or learning how to play a new game, sports-minded people gravitate toward each other. Wear your sweatshirt, baseball cap, or jersey with the name of your team: It's the perfect flirting prop, even if you're at an away game. If you spot someone who could use some athletic tips, what better way to meet than to nonchalantly offer your expertise? Or, if you see someone you like, why not ask for some pointers? All are ideal ways to make the first move.

26. SUPERMARKET, LOCAL MARKET, OR SPECIALTY SHOP

Food: It's the ideal common denominator. What I love most about the supermarket is the overwhelming number of flirting possibilities. In the bakery department, ask a customer what his favorite pastry is. In the produce section, discuss how to pick the perfect melon. If you see someone who needs help, offer your assistance. Take notice of what's in her shopping cart: They are natural conversation starters if you want to find out someone's relationship status. You could say, "Your partner must love fresh veggies," or "Are you going to eat that whole watermelon by yourself?" or "Your husband is going to have a delicious meal."

27. VACATION/TRAVELING

Sightseeing may be the highlight of your vacation, but flirting will add to your memories—and may even last a lifetime! Great ideas for single travelers include singles' cruises, group vacations, solo traveling, or visiting your dream spot in the world.

28. VOLUNTEERING OR CHARITY EVENTS

A shared passion about a cause connects likeminded people to each other. Giving to others lifts your spirits, improves your mood, and enhances your self-esteem. Everyone is on an even playing field with the goal of improving someone else's life. So, take advantage of your heightened self-esteem and positive vibes. Pay it forward with a smile and a warm wink! You'll make someone's day for sure.

29. WAITING IN LINE

We spend endless hours waiting in lines—for the bathroom, at the motor vehicle office, at the movies, return counters, the post office, store checkout lines, and so on. If you are anything like me, you probably want to multitask to make the most of the boring situation. This is where flirting comes in. There are people all around you; you have the time, and you have something in common about which to complain (one of the only times I encourage complaining)! So, don't stand in silence. Start flirting—complain with a smile and start chatting about your purchases.

30. WEDDINGS

Love is in the air at weddings. During the cocktail hour or reception, work the room and introduce yourself to as many people as you can. At your table, make sure you introduce yourself to everyone. If you are single, most likely others at your table will be single as well. If you feel like dancing and don't have a partner, ask someone!

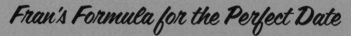

Fran's Formula for the Perfect Date

A great date should:

1 Bring you closer together

2 Offer a shared experience that you both enjoy

3 Help you connect by laughing together

4 Show that you have taken the time to plan something special

TEN FAB DATE IDEAS

The first three dates you have with someone are exciting and nerve-racking at the same time. When it comes to multitasking, dating wins first prize! First, you want to look good, smell delicious, and your place needs to be tidied up just in case your date gets to see your abode. The clock is ticking and you don't want to be late. Once you arrive, you want to be your best self, make a great impression, and keep the conversation going. And then the date is over. Now what? Do you kiss, make plans for another date, or just hope for the best and say good night?

Did I leave anything out? Oh yeah: What to do and where to go! No worries. I'll help you come up with the best-ever date ideas.

But before we do that, think about planning a vacation. You research the best destinations, consider your budget, and come up with a plan that works for you and your traveling companion. Think of your date as a mini-vacation—a little planning goes a long way! Still, please don't obsess about planning the "perfect" date, but do have a "date plan" that will make your date the best it can be.

Also, the amount of money you spend on a date does not necessarily correlate with how successful it will be. In fact, the opposite is often true. A date that costs very little frequently turns out to be the best date imaginable! (BTW, I am not advocating being a cheapskate, or stingy, here: That's a major turn-off.) Consider what might be fun, out of the ordinary (even just a little), inspire conversation, or stir up some romance.

Here are my favorite date ideas. Feel free to tweak, modify, or combine them to make them your own. Whatever you do, put your signature on each date to ensure a fabulous experience—and always remember, *it's just a date*.

1 Be a Tourist in Your Own City

Visit the hot spots, the landmarks, the museums–or even take a tour on an open-air bus or a horse drawn carriage and eat at the tourist traps that are always jam packed. You'll be amazed how much fun it is and you'll be glad you did it. Make sure to take a bunch of photos and selfies as if you were on a real vacation.

2 Go Back to School

You heard me right. Take a class together: yoga, swing dancing, auto mechanics, Photoshop, French, vegan cooking–any class at all, whether it's adult education, at the library, or at the local college or university. As you get to know your date, you'll learn something, too, and it won't have the vibe of an investigative reporter, with a drink in one hand and a mozzarella stick in the other.

Ideal First Dates

DINNER

Try an exotic cuisine, visit a fast-food place you have never been to, or go on a food tour of your city.

DRINKS

Grabbing a drink is a tried-and-true date night classic. Or check out local wineries and breweries.

COFFEE

Sipping on your favorite brew has an easy, relaxed vibe. If you're having a great time, order a second cup.

OUTDOOR ACTIVITY

Full of people having a good time and getting some fresh air— you can't ask for a more positive ambiance!

According to a 2017 survey by Groupon

3 Experience Fabulous Eats

Have brunch at an exclusive hotel or restaurant for a fraction of what dinner costs. Or, restaurant hop: Enjoy appetizers at a tapas place, dessert at a yummy bakery, and a drink at a neighborhood pub. Try an exotic cuisine, visit a fast-food place you have never been to, or go on a food tour of your city—one where the guide takes you to a variety of restaurants. Sample foods at a street festival or simply try the newest restaurant in town.

4 Plan a Surprise Date

I love this idea! Use this when you feel comfortable with your date. Take her on a sort of "blind date." Just tell your date what time to be ready and what the "dress code" is—and you do all the planning. It's the ultimate way to show you care. I've done this before, and my date was ecstatic. I bought tickets to his favorite music group when they were playing at an outdoor venue. What a night we had!

5 Go for Bargains or Freebies

Dating can be expensive, but it doesn't have to be. Check out discount sites such as Groupon that offer great deals on concerts, sports activities, restaurants, massages, and cultural events. You'll find plenty of unusual things to do. For instance, I went to a beautiful lantern festival that was breathtaking—something I never would have done if it weren't a deal. It helped me take a risk! There are other ways to take advantage of free or low-cost events, too: Check out a book launch at a local bookstore; go to a free talk or lecture; or see if your local library offers free passes to museums.

6 Water Is Calming and Connecting

Anything that has to do with water is a great date idea! Taking a ferry ride, going on a moonlit cruise, kayaking, waterskiing, spending a day at the beach or a lake, fishing, frolicking at a water park, or hanging at a pool are all great options. According to Wallace J. Nichols, a marine biologist, "We are hardwired to react positively to water and being near it can calm and connect us." Being around water makes us happier and reduces stress—a perfect reason to include water in your next date.

7 Volunteer Together

Giving back feels good, and a charitable venue is the perfect way to see your date be himself. Whether you love animals, have a passion for the environment, want to give back to the elderly, honor a loved one who has passed, work with disadvantaged kids, or support a cause that needs your help, there are many volunteer opportunities to choose from. Hospitals, shelters, veterans' groups, food pantries, school programs, and political groups always need extra help.

8 Retro Is So Cool

Do you ever wonder if dating was less complicated when your parents or grandparents became an item? Well, why not find out? Turn back the hands of time and have a retro-inspired old-fashioned date. Grab your best socks and go bowling; share a mega-size ice cream sundae; play miniature golf under the stars; get your skates on and go roller skating or ice skating (a great excuse to hold hands!); indulge your sweet tooth at an old-fashioned candy shop; have chocolate fondue; or try your luck at an arcade. All these activities inspire a carefree, relaxed, memorable date!

9 Bars with a Twist

Grabbing a drink with your date is a tried-and-true date night classic. So, how about going to a bar where you can sip your cocktail while playing pool, darts, or trying your hand at painting? Or check out local wineries or breweries. Winetasting and brewery tours enliven both your mind and your palate!

10 Step Out of Your Comfort Zone

Sometimes you just want to throw caution to the wind. Go for it! Soar through the skies in a hot air balloon; rent a fancy car for the evening; go rock climbing, whitewater rafting, or skydiving. These are sure to give you an adrenaline rush—just make sure your date isn't prone to motion sickness or vertigo!

Or, ask your date if there is something he has always wanted to do but never did. Here's your opportunity to try something new and show your date that his interests are important to you. Go to high tea in a hotel; try out an escape room; go to a murder mystery dinner show; visit an obscure museum; find a drive-in; or go to an amusement park. All will give you plenty to talk about—before, during, and, definitely, after the date.

YOUR FLIRTING ENCORE

You've already learned and practiced your online and face-to-face flirting skills as you read this book—even if you were only practicing them in your mind! Now that you're versed in the secret rules of flirting, you are ready to take your flirting expertise into the field. I want you to flirt every day so it continues to be a part of who you are, because flirting, like any other talent, gets better and better with practice.

Whatever you do, don't worry about being perfect. Showing vulnerability and not taking yourself too seriously make you even more desirable. Your increased confidence, your understanding and awareness of the power of your body language, and your ability to talk to anyone at any time in any place will have you looking forward to flirting because you've got the skills to do it.

A terrific way to keep your flirting fresh and exciting is to share your flirting experiences with people who are "flirt challenged." When you talk about your own awkward flirting moments *and* your fabulous flirtatious encounters, you're helping those who need some reassurance. And acting as if you are a flirt extraordinaire will make you feel more confident—and that, in turn, will encourage you to keep stepping out of your comfort zone.

MY WISH FOR YOU

Whenever you flirt, remember I'm right by your side, guiding and encouraging you. If you have a flirting hiccup–and we all do!–know that you learn from every flirting experience you have. And when flirting is a hobby you love, it'll bring more joy and happiness into your life.

Wishing you a future filled with all good things–especially love!

ACKNOWLEDGMENTS

I am so fortunate to have Ken Fund COO of the Quarto Group once again be my cheerleader, and for making *The Secret Rules of Flirting* a reality. Ken, thanks for always making me feel like a star!

My heartfelt gratitude to Jess Haberman, the most amazing, accomplished, and hardworking acquiring editor. You have been my rock, my mentor, my inspiration, and, most importantly, my friend. Thanks for always being there for me and for helping me every step of the way. Your insight, advice, vison, and sense of humor are incredible. I could not have done this without you. I am so lucky to get to work with you on our second book together.

My sincerest kudos to Megan Buckley, my developmental editor who made sure that my voice came alive—and always had the knack to make it better! Thank you for your patience, kindness, and for always being so encouraging and uplifting! I am so glad we were able to work together on our second book! You have a special place in my heart.

A book takes a village and, lucky me, to have the greatest team imaginable. *The Secret Rules of Flirting* was made possible because of the talents of a very gifted group of professionals. I feel so connected to all of you, and words cannot express how thankful and appreciative I am for everything you have done! My warmest thanks to the extraordinary team at Quarto: Publisher, Winnie Prentiss; Associate Publisher, Erika Heilman; Project Editor, Meredith Quinn; Creative Director, Regina Greiner; Art Director, David Martinell; Marketing Manager, Lydia Jopp; Designer, Mattie Wells; and Illustrator, Penelope Dullaghan.

Flirting is in my blood. I live it, breathe it, and love every minute of it. Mom, I learned from the best. I would not be the flirt today if not for you. Your love, charisma, charm, sense of humor, gutsiness, and upbeat attitude touched me to my core. Dad, I loved seeing how you flirted with Mom, the love of your life! You are always with me, and I only wish you could see the incredible impact you have had on my flirting journeys. The tears are welling up as I write this and wish you could see how your flirting has inspired and taught me so much. Thanks for passing on the flirting gene to me so I could share my love of flirting with the world. I love and miss you so much.

I could not have written this book without the love and support of my incredible husband, Dr. James Mullin. A gazillion thanks for always sitting in "the chair" at a moment's notice, listening to every word of the manuscript. Your patience, encouragement, and invaluable input meant the world to me. In your next life, I am sure you will be an editor (you certainly have the experience). Flirting with you from the first day we met has been the happiest times of my life. I wake up every morning wanting to flirt with you. Thank you for always putting a smile on my face and for always singing my praises. For once in my life, I took my own advice and flirted with you the very first time I met you. And because of that, my dream has come true. I love you more today than yesterday and less than tomorrow. Until the next book!

I am truly blessed to have Juliet Gobler in my life. Once again, she has read every word of the manuscript with such meticulousness, offering her take on being single and flirting. Your insight, words of wisdom, and help mean so much to me. I would text Juliet and frantically say, "I need you ASAP." And Juliet would appear! Your generosity, empathy, and kind-heartedness have touched my soul. Love you.

A special thanks to my wonderful friends! You listened, you edited, you cheered me on, you offered advice, and most importantly you helped me get to the finish line: Nancy, Wendy, Roz, Delaina, Daniella, the Carols, Rona, the Mariannes, Kim, Marylou, the Frans, Andi, Harriet, Renee, the Sheilas, Theresa, and Donna.

Huge hugs and appreciation to Trish McDermott, former founding member of Match.com for hiring me and for her continuous inspiration, wisdom, and incredible support.

To my family for always being so reassuring and proud of me, a very special thank you. I love you all.

And, finally, my biggest "thank you" goes to the thousands of workshop participants and clients who have energized, inspired, and taught me so much about the power of flirting. And for everyone I have ever flirted with—you made my day and put a huge smile on my face! Thank you for sharing your flirting triumphs and struggles with me, it is because of you that I have been able to write this book knowing that flirting works! Thank you for allowing me to be a part of your flirting journey.

ABOUT THE AUTHOR

Fran Greene, LCSWR, former director of flirting, advice columnist, and spokesperson for Match.com, is a nationally renowned relationship expert. Flirting is her hobby, love is her passion, and her dream is for you to have a loving relationship. As a flirting coach, she has a private practice in the New York City area working with singles who want to find their perfect match and couples who want to improve their relationship.

Fran is the author of *Dating Again with Courage and Confidence* and *The Flirting Bible*. She is well known as The Flirting, Dating, and Relationship Coach. She is an expert in helping singles navigate the complex maze of online dating and writing winning profiles.

Fran has appeared on the *Today* show, *Jenny McCarthy*, *Dateline NBC*, *Good Day New York*, FIOS 1, *Wingman*, and more. She has been featured in the *Chicago Tribune*, *Wall Street Journal*, *The New York Times*, *Cape Cod Times*, BravoTV.com,

EliteDaily.com, Bustle.com, DatingAdvice.com, Refinery29.com, YourTango.com, Fatherly.com, HerCampus.com, Talkspace.com, *Cosmopolitan*, *Self*, *In Touch Weekly*, and *New York* magazine.

She is also a regular contributor for Zoosk.com.

Fran is known for her insight, gutsiness, humor, and compassion. Through her ever-popular flirting and dating seminars, Fran has helped thousands of people find love. Her 60-Day Dating Action Plan gives you all the dating secrets you need to jumpstart your dating life. Fran's Flirting in the Field Series provides on-the-spot, real-life coaching. She offers powerful, practical, and realistic tips on flirting and dating.

Fran Greene lives in New York with her husband. To contact Fran or to share your greatest flirting moments, visit www.frangreene.com.

INDEX

INDEX